BILL HOGG'S MOST EXCELLENT
GUIDE TO PRAYING

'More things are wrought by prayer,' said an old saint, 'than this world dreams of.' If the two essential corporate conditions of revival are unity and prayer, one of the great hopeful signs of awakening in the western world is a renewed interest in extraordinary prayer. Bill Hogg has done this emerging generation a great service in giving us this collection of practics and principles on prayer. His book is one of the best introductions to prayer by and for the young at the edge of the next millennium.

Winkie Pratney

Bill Hogg's Most Excellent Guide to Praying

BILL HOGG

KINGSWAY PUBLICATIONS
EASTBOURNE

Front cover design by Vic Mitchell

ISBN 0 86065 885 6

Printed in Great Britain for
KINGSWAY PUBLICATIONS LTD
1 St Anne's Road, Eastbourne, E Sussex BN21 3UN by
Clays Ltd, St. Ives plc.
Typeset by Nuprint Ltd, Harpenden, Herts.

To Morag, my wonderful wife
(Proverbs 31:10),
and our little treasures—
Naomi and Peter.

Contents

	Foreword by Steve Chalke	9
	Acknowledgements	11
1.	Dynamite	13
2.	Daddy Dialogue	33
3.	Danger: High Voltage	44
4.	Shut That Door	58
5.	Dead End?	75
6.	Being a Bridge	92
7.	Going by the Book	117
8.	Standing Together	126
9.	Prayer Concerts	136
10.	Prayer Permutations	155
11.	Battleground	172
	Notes	187

Foreword

If you are one of those great prayer warrior types who always finds it easy to pray, is never distracted, and who generally finds being a Christian a bit of a breeze, reading this book is going to be a waste of your time. In fact, my advice is that you either give it away to some less sorted-out Christian in your church who will benefit from its contents or, if you're hard up, return it to the bookshop where you bought it as quickly as you can and try to get your money back!

If on the other hand you're like me, constantly struggling to make your prayer life real (or even to stay awake), then you would be well advised to take the huge step of turning off the telly or whatever else it is that's just about to distract you, and make reading this book a top priority. I've been a Christian for over twenty years, during which time I've constantly struggled to be more like Jesus and to make my prayer life more meaningful and more consistent. I know the Bible tells me to 'pray always', but the truth is that I'm a lot better at talking about the theory of why I should than actually doing much about it.

Bill Hogg's Most Excellent Guide to Praying is not a miracle cure: it won't solve all the problems you face. But if you're anything like me it will be of enormous help.

I commend it to you because I know and respect Bill

Hogg as a down-to-earth, feet-on-the-floor bloke who, like me, struggles to walk with the Lord and is simply seeking to pass on to us the very valuable lessons he has learnt in that struggle. Bill is a great communicator and you will enjoy reading his book—not only because it is well written but, more importantly, because it is practical and honest.

Steve Chalke
The Oasis Trust
London

Acknowledgements

Thanks are due in great heaps to my cousin, Heather McLean, who saved my life as the deadline loomed. She stepped into the breach and put her typing prowess to great use. Thanks also to Mary Pollard and Morag, my wife, who did some of the typing.

Thanks to those in BYFC who have encouraged me with my writing—particularly my good friend, Lowell Sheppard. Special thanks to Morag, my wife and best friend, who put up with me as the deadline loomed, and who constantly supports me and prays for and with me.

Thanks to my prayer supporters who prayed for me and for this project. And thanks to my special prayer supporters, Mum and Dad, who've been praying for me for a l-o-n-g time.

1

Dynamite

It seems like the Beeb bangs it on the box every other Bank Holiday Monday. A true story about POWs who tunnel their way to freedom. It features Steve McQueen and his memorable motorcycle chase. Barbed wire foils his bid for freedom. James Garner, Donald Pleasance, Patrick McGoohan, David McCallum—they're all there. Of course, it's *The Great Escape*.

More recently the movie industry gave us the fictitious *Escape to Victory*. Michael Caine pulls together a POW soccer team, which includes Pelé and Bobby Moore, who take on the Nazis in a French football stadium. The plan is to escape at half-time through a hole in the dressing room bath. However, the Nazis are winning 4-1 at half-time. Caine's crazy cronies decide to go back on the field to win the match. They pull back to 4-4, but seconds away from full-time the referee gives the Germans a penalty. The German forward strikes the penalty well. However, he's not just facing a goalkeeper—the man between the sticks is Sylvester Stallone. Big Sly saves the penalty in slow motion and the stadium erupts. French spectators flood onto the pitch despite the presence of machine-gun-toting stormtroopers, and they give their clothes to the footballers who merge into the crowd and...escape to victory!

Both these films feature a remarkable part of life in a

prisoner-of-war camp—the escape committee. You couldn't just escape whenever it took your fancy. You had to get clearance from the escape committee.

Follow me now as a fly on the wall at an escape committee meeting, where a break-out more spectacular than in any war film is being plotted. The 'Great Escape to Victory' is being strategised in a city centre semi. The committee are listening to instructions:

'I've got a tough assignment for you. The authorities have executed Big Jim. Rocky is currently in detention at Jerusalem Jail. Sixteen soldiers have been assigned to him. He is manacled to two guards in a cell in the punishment block. Our sources indicate he faces a kangaroo court trial once Passover has passed over. He faces certain death. Your mission, should you choose to accept it: spring Rocky from prison. You are his only earthly hope. This tape will self-destruct in five seconds.'

The escape committee have a few options. They can hire a helicopter and drop 'Mad' Mary Magdalene into the prison, armed to the teeth with Uzis and grenades. Bristling with weapons she could blast her way to Simon Peter's cell. However, funds do not permit. Besides, the leader is none too keen on this approach. Neither does he clear Thomas's suggestion to phone the Equaliser. Time does not permit Bartholomew's suggestion of tunnelling in from the city centre sewers to be implemented. Although it is the Feast of Unleavened Bread, Matthias's plan to smuggle Peter out in a baker's delivery van does not have popular approval.

It is Mission Impossible. The escape committee face two options. They can leave Peter at the mercy of a blood-thirsty ruler who would score political points by having him terminated, or...they can use their secret weapon! The great escape plan begins to emerge. Yes, the secret weapon! 'So Peter was kept in prison, but the church was earnestly praying to God for him' (Acts 12:5).

It's the night before trial now. Peter is sound asleep. He has no clothes or blankets. He's wrapped in chains to a guard on either side of him. Suddenly, in the centre of the stinking, stifling cell stands one of God's secret agents. The inky blackness is shattered and scattered by brilliant light. Simon Peter is still in slumberland. The angel thumps Peter. What a flash of heavenly radiance couldn't do, a good belt in the ribs accomplishes. Peter's awake now, all right!

'Quick, get a move on,' the unexpected visitor orders. With a spine-jarring clatter, Peter's chains splinter and fall to the floor.

'Now then, make yourself decent and get your shoes on,' says the decidedly bossy angel: 'Put your coat on— follow me.'

Peter is in a daze, but he has enough sense left in him to obey the angelic instructions. All this stuff is kind of hard to take in, even for an apostle.

'It's got to be a vision,' he mutters.

The angel and the apostle pass two squads of soldiers undetected, and before you can say Simon Bar-Jonah the prison gate swings open *by itself*. City streets! Freedom! They walk down a street together, and then part company.

Perhaps it was the night air that did it, but: 'Then Peter came to himself and said, "Now I know without a doubt that the Lord sent his angel and rescued me from Herod's clutches and from everything the Jewish people were anticipating" ' (Acts 12:11). No wonder Peter's brain had been fog-bound. It was an impossible escape. No dynamite. No tunnel. No wooden horse.

Not only that, in all the war films, when an escape's on, the prisoners blacken their faces and crawl about in the shadows to avoid the searchlights. But, up pops an angel and the floodlights are turned on.

Any film buff worth his salted popcorn will know that

escaping prisoners don't talk—it's hand signals or whispers. The idea is: don't let the guards hear you. Obviously, the angel assigned to Operation Jail-break never watched *The Great Escape*. He barked orders at Peter and started crashing heavy chains on the stone floor! 'For the foolishness of God is wiser than man's wisdom, and the weakness of God is stronger than man's strength' (1 Cor 1:25).

Peter eventually susses out what has happened (being the spiritual sort, an apostle, one of The Twelve and a member of the Big Three) and immediately sets off for his house group meeting. This is where the fun really begins. Peter got out of prison easier than he can get into the prayer meeting!

The place is packed with people praying for Peter. As the church bombards heaven on his behalf, Peter bangs on Mary's door. The meeting is in full swing and there on their doorstep is the very answer to the church's prayers!

Rhoda, Mary's maid, can hear the door being knocked. She slips past John Mark and weaves her way round the very room where, possibly, the Last Supper had been celebrated. Steering her way round kneeling people, prostrate people, people standing with faces and arms heavenward, and seated people, she reaches the hallway. Still the throb of voices urgently pleading for a prisoner can be heard.

'Lord, if it's your will, release your servant from Herod's grasp.'

'Father, keep Peter from danger. Send an angel to protect him.'

'Lord, fill Peter with your peace. Let your love drive out any fears in his heart.'

Suddenly the prayer is interrupted by an excited chattering.

'It's Peter—he's at the door! Peter's here!'

How do the prayer warriors receive the joyful news? A

host of hallelujahs? A praise party? Do they whip out their guitars for a burst of 'All Glory Be To Thee?' Not exactly....

'Don't be so stupid, Rhoda.'

'But I tell you—it's Peter. I'd know his accent any-where.'

'Look, Rhoda, it must be his angel. Peter's probably dead by now.'

While the identity of the person on the doorstep is debated, Peter continues to thump his bruised fist on the door. Finally, someone has the bright idea that opening the front door should settle the issue. So, there he is— Peter! And 'their surprise knew no bounds' (Acts 12:16, TLB). Peter fills the astonished crowd in on his escape and then goes off into hiding.

This little episode, recorded by Dr Luke in Acts 12:1– 19, teaches us a number of things about the mysterious secret weapon every Christian has at his or her disposal: prayer.

Prayer is supernatural dynamite

Prayer releases the explosive, supernatural power of God into impossible situations. The impossible jail-break took place because God's people prayed. Peter had earned a reputation as a jail-breaker (see Acts 5:17–26) and was placed in maximum security. Humanly speaking there was no way out. But the church prayed and God stepped in.

Jesus promises, '...if you have faith as small as a mus-tard seed, you can say to this mountain, "Move from here to there" and it will move. Nothing will be impossible for you' (Mt 17:20). But the pray-er's ministry of mountain moving does not rest on the bigness of our faith. It is true that 'without faith it is impossible to please God' (Heb 11:6). But prayer is not a case of 'having enough faith' and 'saying the right words'. Augustine said, 'We may pray most when we say least, and we may pray least when we say most.'

Those Christians in Mary's house meeting were urgent and energetic in their praying, but clearly did not operate at a high faith level. When Peter—the very answer to their prayers—stood at the door, they refused to accept Rhoda's excited reports. R. A. Torrey reckoned that the reason Rhoda gets a mention is because, out of the lot of them, Rhoda is the one who prayed believingly.

The Christians' faith was weak and feeble, but God answered. They had very little faith, but they were praying to a great and mighty God. The good news is that God answers prayers of paste and flour as well as prayers of faith and power! The good news is that the explosive power of prayer rests in the bigness of God. God is far greater than our faith. He is bigger than our prayers.

Doubtless, this is what Bishop Michael Baughen had in mind when he said, 'Prayer cannot change Britain, but the God who answers prayer can.' Prayer has powerful potential because our God is all-powerful. The root of success in prayer is the bigness of God—not the bigness of our praying. Prayer succeeds because God is a God of love, mercy, might, holiness, majesty and power.

An unknown poet wrote:

Satan laughs at the words we say;
Smiles at our efforts from day to day,
But Satan *trembles* when he sees
The *weakest* saint upon his knees.

Guy H. King tells us, 'No one is a firmer believer in the power of prayer than the devil; not that he practises it, but he suffers from it.'

We are weak. Jesus informs us, 'Apart from me you can do nothing' (Jn 15:5). The good news is that his strength is

made perfect in our weakness. When we bend our knees—
and, more importantly, our hearts—in prayer, we
become channels of the supernatural power of God. We
become people who can change history. As Winkie
Pratney writes: 'Prayer is the vast, little known and little
explored power which moves the arm of God, which shakes
nations, binds hell and accomplishes the impossible.'[1]

'Tremendous power is made available through a good
man's earnest prayer' (Jas 5:16, PHILLIPS).

- Moses prayed and the Red Sea opened up and became
  an escape route for the Israelites.
- Moses held up his hands in prayer on the hilltop and
  the Amalekites were routed in battle.
- Joshua prayed and the sunset was delayed for a day!
- Hannah prayed and God gave her a son.
- Elijah prayed and there was no rain and no dew for
  three-and-a-half years.
- Elijah prayed and God sent fire from heaven.
- Elijah prayed and the drought ended.
- Daniel prayed and the lunchtime lions' jaws were clamp-
  ed.
- Shadrach, Meschach and Abednego prayed and God
  visited them in the furnace.
- The 120 prayed and the Spirit of God came down from
  heaven in hurricane power, and they turned the world
  upside-down for Jesus.
- Paul prayed and was famous in hell.

As Screwtape remarked, 'Real prayer is lethal.' And
Billy Kim thundered at the Christian conference Amster-
dam '86, 'Prayer does not need proof—it needs practice.'

When Jesus gave us the disciples' prayer pattern and
taught us to pray, 'Your kingdom come', he was teaching
us that real prayer is inviting a royal power invasion from
heaven!

Revelation 8:4–5 reveals the devastating power that prayer has when it is ignited by the fire of God.

The smoke of the incense, together with the prayers of the saints, went up before God from the angel's hand. Then the angel took the censer, filled it with fire from the altar, and hurled it on the earth; and there came [here are the results, folks] peals of thunder, rumblings, flashes of lightning and an earthquake.

Prayer to the God of heaven is supernatural dynamite because it effects explosive change in the here and now.

All heaven waits with baited breath,
For saints on earth to pray.
Majestic angels ready stand
With swords of fiery blade
Astounding power awaits a word
From God's resplendent throne
But God awaits our prayer of faith,
That cries 'Your will be done.'

Awake, O Church, arise and pray,
Complaining words discard!
The Spirit comes to fill your mouth
With truth His mighty sword.
Go place your feet on Satan's ground
And there proclaim Christ's name;
In step with heaven's armies march
To conquer and to reign!

Now in our hearts and on our lips
The word of faith is near.
Let heaven's will on earth be done,
Let heaven flow from here!
Come blend your prayers with Jesus' own,
Before the Father's throne;

And as the incense clouds ascend
God's holy fire rains down!

All heaven waits Graham Kendrick and
Chris Rolinson © Thank You Music 1986.

Prayer is hard work and urgent business

There's a world of difference between saying prayers and praying. Praying means unleashing God's dynamite, but praying also means sweating. It is an active, energy-sapping, grappling with God. It means engaging the forces of darkness in spiritual combat. Prayer is warfare. For Jacob, prayer was a wrestling match where he cried out to God, 'I'm not letting you go till you bless me!'

Jesus prayed in the Garden of Gethsemane, and his praying was an awful, agonising experience. Sweat drops like blood fell from his brow as he wrestled in prayer. 'And being in anguish, he prayed more *earnestly*' (Lk 22:44, italics mine). Dr Luke uses the same word to describe Jesus' praying and the church's praying for Peter (*ektenōs*).

If you've got a King Jimmy (sorry, that's my affectionate name for a King James Bible) you'll notice that it translates Acts 12:5 as '...prayer was made *without ceasing* unto God for him [Peter].' This word in italics means 'stretched-out-edly'. The King James translators saw it as extended prayer, ie, over a period of time. Acts 12 reveals that prayer went up to God over an extended period. But here the word means stretched-out-edly like putting someone on a rack! The actual thrust of Acts 12:5 is prayer was going on with 'intense earnestness' (WEYMOUTH). The church was on the rack for Peter! Their praying was no holy hobby or pious pastime—it was hard work and urgent business.

Our praying needs to display this kind of spiritual aggro. We need to go for it with guts and gusto when we pray.

'It is not how long we pray, or how we choose our words—it's our level of urgency that counts. We must not only pray; we must pray fervently with great urgency and intensity. We must not only pray; we must storm heaven's gates with unfaltering persistence. It is this type of prayer that has changed whole societies and destroyed satanic influence over the years.'[2]

We need to be stickers

I'm quite sure that the church started praying as soon as Peter was arrested. However, his handcuffs did not immediately evaporate! He was thrown in prison and spent several days there. Prayer involves asking God and seeking him, but it can mean that to see results, we have to commit ourselves to persistent knocking! Mary's house group didn't see instant results. Perhaps that's why hopes had flagged, and they'd had such a hard time handling Rhoda's insistence that God had sprung a jail-break!

We've got instant coffee, instant potatoes (yuk), instant porridge—but God does not guarantee instant 'just-ask, Amen' answers to prayer. Jesus instructs us to pray and not give up (Lk 18:1).

Your friend pops round to borrow suppertime supplies for a surprise midnight guest. You're tucked up in bed. The doorbell brings you out of slumberland. You try to turn over. The doorbell screams at you. It's cold outside the confines of your king-size quilt.

You're not getting up because it's your friend that's at the door. You're getting up because his thumb's glued to the doorbell, and you don't want the rest of the house waking up. His persistence has paid off—he walks home clutching three Mother's Prides.

God is not some kind of semi-conscious, grumpy friend that we bully out of bed to give us bread (Lk 11:7–8). Prayer is not breaking down God's reluctance—it's taking hold of his willingness. But we need to persist in prayer, to ask and go on asking, to seek and go on seeking, and to knock and go on knocking.

A wicked, nasty dad won't give his boy a scorpion supper if he wants fish and chips, and bad Dad won't give his wee daughter a rock to chew or a stone to suck if she wants a boiled egg for breakfast. It's in the context of his teaching on prayer that Jesus tells us bad dads know how to give good gifts, and he adds, '...how much more will your Father in heaven give the Holy Spirit to those who ask him!' (Lk 11:13).

Our Father is a how-much-more God! If a self-centred, bigoted, atheistic judge responds to a widow who badgers him for justice, how much more will God do right by his chosen ones (Lk 18:1–8)? The parable *contrasts* our loving Father God, who welcomes our cries, with an unjust judge whose resistance has to be worn away.

We need to be stickers because sometimes we will encounter fierce, supernatural opposition to our praying. Daniel discovered this (see Daniel 10). We need to be stickers, because prayer is not some kind of magic lamp where we rub it and up pops an angel ready to follow our every command.

God can say yes to our prayer requests, but he can also say no, and he may say wait. He is our all-loving Father, but that does not mean he answers yes all the time. Earthly dads often say no because of their love. Little children may enjoy playing in the middle of the street, but Dad knows it's a place of danger. Our Father responds in the way that fits our *ultimate* good (Rom 8:28), and grants us all our *needs* but not our greeds (Phil 4:19).

Peter's prayer back-up team in Acts 12 were persistent pray-ers. We need to learn from them.

We must learn to pray in the will of God

> Prayer is not an argument with God to persuade him to move things our way, but an exercise by which we are enabled by His Spirit to move ourselves His way.
>
> LEONARD RAVENHILL

Sometimes we pray like Aladdin, doing our lamp rubbing. We need to learn to pray like Jesus: 'Not my will, Father, but yours.' Jesus taught us to pray, 'Your kingdom come and your will be done on earth as it is in heaven.' Prayer involves discerning the will of God in a situation and then going for it. We hear from him first, and then we launch out in believing prayer. Jesus said, 'If you remain in me and my words remain in you, ask whatever you wish, and it will be given you' (Jn 15:7).

Jesus presents us with a blank cheque signed by him: '...my Father will give you whatever you ask in my name. Until now you have not asked for anything in my name. Ask and you will receive, and your joy will be complete' (Jn 16:23–24).

As Luis Palau says, Jesus invites us to 'pray great prayers'. This praying involves walking close to Jesus, hearing his voice—his desires being our desires—and involves us in praying in line with the will of God.

When we know we are praying in line with the purposes of God, we're on to a winner! The church in Acts 12 could have prayed with unshakable confidence and aggressive boldness if they had got hold of Jesus' words about Peter in John 21:18. Prayer is claiming the promises of God. Prayer is challenging God to be faithful to his word. 'Real prayer is taking His Word into the Throne Room and letting His words speak through your lips to Him on the throne, calling His attention to His own promises.'[3]

> Jesus said...'I tell you the truth, when you were younger you dressed yourself and went where you wanted; but when you

are old you will stretch out your hands, and someone else will dress you and lead you where you do not want to go.' Jesus said this to Peter to indicate the kind of death by which Peter would glorify God (Jn 21:18–19).

The church could come to God and say, 'Peter's not old. You say he'd be a ripe old age when he died. Set him free, Lord!'

Perhaps it was this very promise that allowed Peter to enjoy a deep sleep the night before he was to be put to death. Resting in prison on the promise of Jesus! God's promises are sure. Our praying needs to be fuelled and fired and faith-ed up (see Romans 10:17) by the word of God.

P.R.A.Y.E.R. for others

The early church's urgent praying was doubtless fuelled by a deep concern for Peter. He had buckled under pressure before. He had denied and disowned Jesus when the going got tough. They loved Peter, so they prayed for Peter. We need to pray with the flame of God's love burning within us.

It is easy for our praying to orbit around me, myself and I, and my needs and my aspirations. We need to pray for those around us, those in need. Peter was in desperate need. The church urgently prayed for him. Acts 12:5 does *not* read, 'Peter was kept in prison, so the church was earnestly crying out to God for strength to cope in the absence of its leader.'

Our prayer life has to extend to the hurting, the downtrodden, the broken-hearted, the lost and the sick. We need to invite the Holy Spirit to give us praying hearts filled with God's love (Rom 5:5), and to invite him to give us God's heart—a heart that experiences grief and pain (Gen 6:6).

Prayer means passion! 'During the days of Jesus' life on

earth, he offered up prayers and petitions with loud cries and tears...' (Heb 5:7). As we draw near to God and pray for others and their needs, we run the risk of becoming people of loud cries and tears. Praying Hyde was an extraordinary man who knew what extraordinary prayer was. Doctors discovered that his heart had moved. His physical flesh and blood pump under his chest had moved because of the intensity of his praying! We need to have hearts that are moved to pray extraordinary prayers.

Evangelist Roy Crowne says, 'PRAYER is Please Remember Always Your End Result.' Prayer must be specific. The church had a specific prayer target: Peter (Acts 12:5).

We can do better than 'God bless the world, God bless the missionaries, Amen' praying. Praying like that is so fuzzy we don't know whether or not God has answered! Fuzzy prayers are safe—no risks are involved because their vagueness rules out the need for faith. You only see answered prayer in response to specific prayer!

Make your praying faith-sized

We need to pray within the scope of our faith. There's no point asking God to save all of Puddleton-upon-the-Sea if we don't believe he can save the person who sits next to us in Geography.

Some of the Acts 12 prayer warriors ran into trouble because they were praying outside the boundaries of their faith. If they'd been engaged in faith-sized praying they wouldn't have given Rhoda such stick!

An unsaved family moved next door to a French missionary. He duly wrote them into his prayer-notebook and began praying that they would be converted. After months of prayer, nothing had happened, so the missionary cried out, 'Lord, why haven't you saved my neighbour?'

'Because you don't believe it,' the Lord responded.

'But Lord, nothing's too difficult for you.'

'I know that, but you don't believe it.'

'But Lord, nothing is impossible for you.'

'I know that, but you don't believe it. Can you imagine your neighbours being converted?'

'No,' replied the French missionary.

'Stop praying for what you can't imagine happening.'

'Well, Lord, what can I pray for?' asked the missionary.

'Pray for something you can imagine happening.'

The missionary prayed, 'Lord, I'd really like to have a chat with my neighbour—within a week.'

Thursday arrived and both men spent the evening gardening. It wasn't long before they were chatting over the fence. The missionary's faith grew.

'Lord, I'd really like to get inside his house.'

It wasn't long before Mr and Mrs Missionary were invited next door for coffee. Mr Missionary's faith grew.

'Lord, I pray *he* brings up the subject of religion.'

When Mr and Mrs Missionary popped next door for coffee their neighbour asked, 'Where do you go every Sunday at ten o'clock like clockwork?'

'Church,' responded Mr Missionary.

'Why?' enquired Mr Next-door-neighbour. They were into a great discussion, and Mr Missionary's faith grew even more.

'Lord, I pray that I can introduce him to some of my Christian friends.' And he did!

'Lord, I pray that he'll come to church.' And he did!

'Lord, save my neighbour.' And he did![4]

Like the French missionary, we need to learn to pray with faith-sized objectives. We need to be specific and faith-sized pray-ers because Jesus asks us, 'What do you want me to do for you?' Just as he posed the question to the blind beggar outside Jericho (Lk 18:35–43), he poses it to us now.

Prayer changes people

The power of prayer is not impeded by geography. As we learn to pray we can become global people of God, interceding for people who don't even know us! We can be involved in events thousands of miles away. We can bring change into situations, and into people who are far from us. As we commit ourselves to be people of prayer the Spirit of God will take us beyond the cosy confines of our prayer closets and involve us in others' lives.

I already said that Peter slept in his cell because of the security of Jesus' prophecy in John 21. I also believe that he was enjoying his beauty sleep because praying Christians had prayed that God's word would become real in Peter's experience. Praying Christians got involved in Peter's situation and released faith and the peace of Jesus into his life. His sleep was so deep, the angelic intruder had to punch him to get him moving!

Herod had a grisly death lined up for Peter, but Peter enjoyed the peace that 'passes all understanding'. Your prayers make a difference.

Peter had caved in under pressure before, but Jesus' prayers prevented Peter from totally losing his grip (see Luke 22:31ff).

Herod plots. Christians pray. Peter is secure in his God and sleeps like a baby.

Prayer sets the captives free and releases supernatural light into darkness

Light shattered the darkness; Peter was freed from his chains and released from prison because Christians set themselves to pray.

But your workplace, your school, your street is filled with prisoners. Your factory, your dole queue, your town is packed with people in darkness. 'The god of this age has blinded the minds of unbelievers, so that they cannot see the light of the gospel of the glory of Christ, who is the image of God' (2 Cor 4:4).

'Evangelism is regaining territory that has been taken by the enemy. It is not a process of intellectually convincing people of truth but of releasing them from prison.'[5]

If we are to see people released from the grip of sin and set free from the kingdom of darkness, we must engage in prayer warfare. Pray that God will shine light from heaven into enemy strongholds and into darkened lives. We need to pray that the Holy Spirit will pull back the curtains and reveal Jesus to those we know are lost. Make your non-Christian friends (or enemies) your prayer targets. John Wesley was a fiery evangelist who set England alight spiritually two centuries ago. He knew the secret of fruitful evangelism: 'God does nothing except in response to prayer.' Thousands of people came into the kingdom in a mighty move of the Holy Spirit. Why? Because of anointed preaching, *yes*. But why was it anointed? Because of *agonised praying*!

We need to pray that Jesus will smash the chains that hold people captive. Then we'll hear them sing to Jesus:

Long my imprisoned spirit lay
Fast bound in sin and nature's night;
Thine eye diffused a quickening ray,
I woke, the dungeon flamed with light;
My chains fell off, my heart was free;
I rose, went forth and followed Thee.[6]

Through prayer we can see the darkness scatter, see the chains that bind people smashed, see the captives enjoy liberty, and see the grip of evil broken!

Prayer is a protest

Evil was triumphing. Herod wanted blood—Peter's! The church could have sat back and wailed, 'Poor Peter, he's had it—he's history.' But the church activated its secret weapon against evil: prayer. Prayer is our protest against evil. Prayer is a threat against the forces of darkness. We can come to Father and make our protests. 'Lord, things have gone far enough. Bring change. Bring truth and justice.'

Ian Savory, Director of Norwich Youth For Christ, once told me the story of One-eyed Jack. Jack was a drunkard who got converted and became a man ablaze for Jesus. Jack was a real prayer warrior and served Jesus as an officer in the Salvation Army. He wore red trousers with the following inscription on the backside: 'Where will you spend eternity: heaven or hell?' To draw a crowd, One-eyed Jack would climb up a lamppost and ring bells. When he got his crowd he preached the gospel! A local bylaw was going to be passed to prevent the Salvation Army from marching. Jack and his soldiers marched straight to the town hall where they staged a prayer sit-in. The Army won!

One-eyed Jack would get really uptight about the damage done to people in the drinking houses. So Jack would pray them shut, and he would inform the owners that they could close down and cut their losses or go down in disgrace.

A popular gin-house song was: 'Here's to the good old whisky, knock it down.' Jack liked the tune but changed the words to: 'Storm the forts of darkness, bring them down.' Prayer is 'storming the forts'.

Liberal MP David Alton popped up at Spring Harvest 1988. He received a standing ovation at a youth meeting there where he spoke about his battle against the evil of abortion. Some of his opponents commented on 'Alton's dirty tricks'. David Alton informed us his opponents were referring to Christians praying in support of his bill. We need to engage in the dirty tricks department and be a people who make our protests against evil before God's throne.

One preacher I heard suggested Christians should turn their newspapers into prayer lists! We should be very much aware of current events and pray that God's kingdom would come into these situations, and where there is evil and injustice to pray against it.

Allan Boesak, veteran anti-apartheid campaigner, points the way for Christians to combat the blasphemy of apartheid:

> If the rulers will not hear the cries of the people, if they will not change, if they continue to prevent justice, let us pray them out of existence. God will hear our cry.... We do not believe in the power of violence, but we do believe in the power of prayer.[7]

To be effective prayer-protestors we need holy anger. The Bible says, 'Be angry but do not sin' (Eph 4:26, RSV). We need to pray for a baptism of holy anger so that we might defeat evil in our praying. God wants people who will be aggressive against evil. 'All it takes for evil to triumph is for good men to do nothing.' We *can* do something! We can pray!

Prayer is two-way communication

I've mentioned more than once the ice-cool reception Rhoda got when she told the escape committee that God's man was on the loose. Part of the reason must lie in the pray-ers not grasping that prayer is two-way communication. We can speak to God. If we stop and listen, God will speak to us! Jesus said, 'My sheep hear my voice' (Jn 10:27, KJV). God says, 'Call unto me, and I will answer...' (Jer 33:3, KJV).

George Muller was labelled 'an apostle of faith'. He saw remarkable answers to prayer. Hugh Black recounts one such instance:

> George Muller was due to preach in the United States. However, he found himself delayed through fog as he crossed the Atlantic. Muller had no doubt of God's will with regard to the preaching engagement, but time began to press. The ship's Captain was a Christian and the two men went to his cabin to pray...From the cabin the weather conditions could not be observed. The Captain was of the opinion Muller could not arrive on time. Muller prayed and by faith accepted the removal of the fog. The Captain was about to pray when Muller stopped him, saying, 'Don't you pray. In the first place you don't believe that God will move the fog and in the second place there is no need, since He has already done so.' They went on deck. The fog was gone. Muller fulfilled his engagement. You see, Muller walked sufficiently close to God to hear His voice. He knew he should accept the appointment. He knew God makes no mistakes. He believed he would be on time. He would hear the whisper in the cabin that the fog was gone. It would not be difficult for him to believe it. He lived that way.[8]

2

Daddy Dialogue

They sit in the burger bar. His quarter-pounder with cheese sits cold and unfinished. Rigor mortis claimed her french fries long ago. Films strong enough to trampoline on lie across the surface of their coffees. Arms extend over the table, hands meet, fingers interlock. They gaze, unblinking like fish, into the respective windows of their souls. Their intimate silence is occasionally punctuated by a sigh. The roof could cave in, the walls crumble, the deep fat fryer incinerate. They would not blink or budge. They have entered another dimension. They have entered the Twilight Zone. Their anthem is that oldie, 'I Only Have Eyes For You'. They delight in one another's company. 'Two hearts together in just one mind, beating together till the end of time.' They will tell you, 'We're in love.' Painful puppy love? It may well be, but their mutual affection means they want to be together.

If a man and woman love one another they will enjoy each other's company. They will take time for one another and delight in getting alone together. I love my wife, Morag, and I'm happy to report that Morag loves me. I enjoy her company. It's great when I'm at home and our children, Naomi and Peter, are tucked up in bed. Then we can have each other to ourselves! It's great doing things when it is just the two of us. We are husband and wife. We are the best of friends. We made a commitment to each other—we got married. But to enjoy a marriage relationship it is not enough just to say, 'I do', at a wedding. One of the keys in a marriage is keeping open lines of communication and spending time together.

God is looking for people who will cultivate a love relationship with him. If you are a Christian you have made a commitment to Jesus Christ. You said, 'I do'. You said, 'Jesus I do want to follow you. I do want you to be king of my life. I surrender to you.' However, it does not end there—it's just the beginning! Prayer is a means of developing that relationship. Prayer produces intimacy with God. It means engaging in the romance of redemption.

Jesus told his disciples, 'I have called you friends, for everything that I learned from my Father I have made known to you' (Jn 15:15). If you are a genuine Christian, Jesus is your best friend. Prayer deepens that friendship. Jesus love us and longs for us to draw aside and deepen our friendship with him. And it is in that place of intimacy that we get to know God. To enjoy God as our Father and to really know him as our friend we need to spend time in his presence. Simply waiting on him, loving and adoring him, pursuing relationship with him.

In Chapter 6, Being a Bridge, we will examine the ministry of intercession that God has called us to and look at some snapshots of Moses the mighty prayer warrior. But Moses didn't just clock up prayer time on behalf of Israel. He did pray prayers that damaged Satan's kingdom. But he also spent time in prayer because he enjoyed friendship with God. Moses had a tent he used to get alone with God in. He would get away from the buzz of Israel's community life and pitch the tent. He met with God, poured out his heart to God, and heard from heaven. Scripture records, 'The Lord would speak to Moses face to face, as a man speaks with his friend' (Ex 33:11).

God would speak to Moses in 'the tent of meeting'. Prayer was not a monologue for Moses. He did not fill the tent with hot air and words. Prayer for Moses was a dialogue. Prayer is a conversation between two friends.

Our priority as disciples of Jesus must be intimacy with God. This was Paul's cry: 'I want to know Christ...' (Phil 3:10). This was not the cry of an unconverted man stumbling around in spiritual darkness. It was the heart cry of a converted, Spirit-filled, mature man of God. He wanted to know Jesus in a deeper way.

He was echoing the psalmist's desire:

As the deer pants for streams of water,
So my soul pants for you, O God.
My soul thirsts for God, for the living God.
When can I go and meet with God? (Ps 42:1–2).

You have an open invitation to 'go and meet with God'. It was the psalmist's longing to commune with God. Are you thirsty for God? Do you want a deeper relationship with Jesus? Perhaps you don't have much of a spiritual thirst. Maybe you're saying, 'I'm cold. I feel like a lump of granite.' Ask God to give you a desire for intimacy with him. The Bible tells us twice that 'Enoch walked with God', and also that 'Noah walked with God'. God's desire is for people who walk with him and talk with him. He wants you to draw aside and enjoy unbroken communion with him.

God wants us to open our hearts to experience his friendship. Jesus says, 'My sheep hear my voice' (Jn 10:27, KJV). We need to take time to tune in and hear what God wants to speak into our lives for today. 'Today, if you hear his voice, do not harden your hearts...' (Ps 95:7–8). Prayer is not rushing down on to our knees and pouring out words to God. Prayer is a dialogue—a conversation. God wants to hear from you—he loves to listen to his children talk to him. He also wants to speak into your life.

How much room is there in your life for conversation with God?

Read through and chew over Luke 10:38—42 and its implications for your life. Many Christians are Marthas sucked into a whirlpool of activism, instead of Marys making friendship with Jesus a priority, and talking and listening to him. God wants you to be a house of prayer. God does not want an army of cop-outs. The remedy for frantic activism is not impersonating a statue. God wants you to get your hands dirty, to serve him and serve others.

The issue is priorities. The issue is pace. Does the pace of your schedule make room for developing your relationship with your Lord and Saviour? When we get our priorities upside down we become cranky like Martha (Lk 10:40). We become worried, uptight and upset (Lk 10:41). If we don't put first things first like Mary did (Lk 10:42), we will have a distorted perspective on life and an impoverished Christian experience.

God is not into breeding bone idle Christians. But he does want us to be worshippers before we are workers. Mary chose what was better—she sat in submission to Jesus, focusing on and listening to him.

Prayer is our communication system with the Father. How operational is your communication system?

The *Titanic* was reputed to be the unsinkable ship. However, despite the outrageous claim that even God could not sink her, she was lost on her maiden voyage back in 1912. The *Titanic* scraped an iceberg which ripped her hull, and she was lost in the Atlantic.

The tragedy is that the vessel acknowledged receiving six ice warnings via the wireless. These ice warnings indicated an ice field seventy-eight miles long was directly ahead of the ship. However, the radio operators who received the ice warnings were civilians. Jack Phillips and his junior, Harold Bride, were employed by British Marconi Company. These men were not part of the established shipboard chain of command. There was no routine procedure for them to follow in the delivery of messages to the bridge. The transmitting and receiving apparatus were in fine working order. But the messages were not relayed and acted upon. And the successive ice warnings were disregarded.

The *Californian* was a ship encompassed by an ice field. She sent an ice report in the afternoon of April 14. Bride did not record the report. Phillips delayed acting on information that affected the ship's course. The 'unsinkable' *Titanic* sank on the evening of Sunday April 14, 1912. There had been a breakdown in the communication system.

Prayer is your communication system with God. Many Christians are struggling and sinking because of a breakdown in communications with the captain of their salvation.

You don't earn gold stars if you clock up lots of time praying. God's love for you is completely unconditional. God loves you irrespective of your commitment to use the communications system. He does not love you more if you spend lots of time praying. He does not love you any less if you observe 'radio silence'.

Genesis 4:1 informs us, 'And Adam knew Eve his wife; and she conceived...' (KJV). We are also told, '...the people that do know their God shall be strong, and do exploits' (Dan 11:32b). The same word is used to describe both Adam's sexual intimacy with his wife and knowing God. The word is *yada*. The secret of gaining holy boldness and doing exploits for God is in intimate fellowship with God in prayer. Adam's and Eve's intimacy resulted in life—Eve conceived. Cultivating intimate fellowship with God results in an infusion of life. In the place of prayer the child of God experiences a life exchange. 'But those who wait for the Lord...shall change and renew their strength and power...' (Is 40:30, AMPLIFIED).

When my daughter Naomi was a toddler, she would often come up to me and say, 'Knee, Daddy, knee.' I could have been in my office, or parked on the settee. She wanted me to lift her up, plop her on my knee, and snuggle her close. Great! She's four-and-a-half as I write this. Sometimes she'll come up to her mum or me and announce, 'I want a cuddle.' Peter, her brother, is six months old—he cannot verbalise his requests to be snuggled. Sometimes he'll lift up his arms so that we get the message. 'Pick me up! I want a hug!'

Father God delights in his children turning to him and crying, 'Knee, Daddy, knee.' He longs for us to nestle into him. You don't have to be great with words to express your love to God. Praise and adoration should be a feature of your prayer menu.

The Lord's Prayer, as we label it, involves an invitation to worship and adore. It involves praising Father God. 'Our Father who is in heaven, hallowed be your name.' Spend time praising God. A preacher entered a building where the kids were cockney. They were singing an old hymn: 'Prize him for his grace and favour....' Prize instead of praise. But they got it right! Praise involves prizing God, expressing our appreciation to him vocally. If you prize something you value it.

Jacob was a bit of a twister in the Old Testament. He was always working an angle. He brought his 'what's in it for me' philosophy into his praying.

> Then Jacob made a vow, saying, 'If God will be with me and will watch over me on this journey I am taking and will give me food to eat and clothes to wear so that I return safely to my father's house, then the Lord will be my God...' (Gen 28:20–21).

Evangelist Luis Palau has called Jacob 'the schemer'. He tried to bring his scheming into his relationship with God. God delights in meeting our needs, but prayer is not a scheme for getting things from God. Prayer should not be, 'Gimme, gimme'. True prayer will involve expressing our love to God. True prayer will involve offering thanksgiving to God. It means spending time enjoying God. 'Enter his gates with thanksgiving and his courts with praise; give thanks to him and praise his name' (Ps 100:4). Spend time singing to the Lord. Sing songs, hymns or choruses that express your love to God. King David said, 'Sing a new song to the Lord.' Make up songs of praise and thanksgiving. Spend time enjoying God for who he is and vocalise your joy.

Prayer is a conversation between you and God. That means you should take time to listen to God. You can talk to God anywhere, any time—that's your privilege if you are one of the kids of the King. He also wants to talk to you. So, build listening time in—enjoy dialogue with your heavenly Daddy. A. W. Tozer said, 'The man who would know God must spend time with him.'

In this book we will explore different aspects of prayer. We will look at prayer frameworks and models for corporate prayer. But, I want to encourage you to engage in conversational prayer. Pray to enjoy God! Spend time silently absorbing his love. Take time to hear him for yourself. The Israelites said to Moses, 'You speak to us, and we will hear; but let not God speak to us, lest we die' (Ex 20:19, RSV). Israel was quite content to let Moses be a middle man. They did not want God to speak directly into their lives. You don't have to settle for that! Jesus brings us into the presence of his Father; he has opened up permanent access and lines of communication to the Father. It's great to listen to Christian tapes, get into good Christian books, attend Christian festivals and conferences. But you do not need an evangelical guru to filter the voice of God through to you. God *can* speak to you through preachers, face to face, or via video or audio cassettes. God *can* encourage you and challenge you through what you read. But don't let these blessings rob you of your right as a child of God to hear from your Father in heaven.

Paul said, 'Pray without ceasing' (1 Thess 5:17, KJV). Surely he could not have been serious? 'God really can't expect me to pray non-stop, can he?' you ask. Prayer is an attitude of dependence on God. Your prayer life flows out of your relationship with God.

This brings me to a vital issue: is God your Father? Have you had a revolutionary Jesus experience? Do you have a personal relationship with God? If you have not entered into a genuine relationship with God, you cannot pray. If praying is a Father/child dialogue, you have to be part of God's family to get on the communications system. If you're reading this book, it will almost certainly mean you are religious. However, God does not require us to be religious. You have to be 'born from above' (Jn 3:3, JERUSALEM BIBLE). You need to receive new life from the Holy Spirit.

John Wesley said:

Go to church twice a day. Go to the Lord's table every week. Say as many prayers in private as you can pray. And then listen to all the sermons you care to hear. Read all the books you can read about Christ. Still you must be born again.[9]

A. W. Tozer wrote in his book, *When He is Come*:

So it is that the human being can know about God, he can know about Christ's dying for him, he can even write songs and books, be the head of religious organisations and hold important church offices and still never come to a vital, personal knowledge of God at all. Only by the Holy [Spirit] can he know God.[10]

Do you know God? Do you have a definite, personal, intimate friendship with him? If you are not an authentic follower of Jesus, you can't be on real speaking terms with God. It's not enough to put your mitt in the air and say, 'I believe in Jesus.' A Christian isn't just someone who believes in Jesus. A Christian has been changed by Jesus and is committed to following him.

Jesus taught us to pray, 'Our Father...'. A personal relationship with God is foundational. It is the cornerstone on which a life of prayer is built. Prayer is not a legalistic formula that we recite. Prayer is not a matter of words. Prayer overflows out of that child/Father relationship with God that Jesus made possible by his sacrifice for us.

To gain access to the Father we come through Jesus. There is no other means of access to God. We can come to God purely on the basis of what Jesus has done for us. Jesus lived a life of perfect obedience to his Father. Jesus died for our sins on our behalf. He was raised from the dead and lives for ever, and you can enjoy his resurrection—jail-break life. 'He was delivered over to death for our sins and was raised to life for our justification' (Rom 4:25).

Sin is the stuff that makes God deaf to your prayers. Have you been to Jesus for cleansing and experienced forgiveness? Have you let go of the wrong in your life?

I recently had breakfast in McDonald's. As I entered this famous eats place, I spotted a sign. People on skateboards, and people with rollerskates and no shirts, could not enter. They could not have their tastebuds tickled by a Big Mac. They could not sample the glorious Egg McMuffin. Restricted personnel only! McDonald's is no five star establishment, but to gain entrance you have to observe protocol.

God's throne room has a sign above it. There is restricted access to God—authorised personnel only. Christians revel in the immanence of God, that God is everywhere. But we also need to get hold of the fact that he is 'totally other'. He is holy and righteous. He hates sin and darkness. Only children of the living God have unrestricted access to the Father. Are you one of the King's kids?

John writes about Jesus and tells us:

Yet to all who received him, to those who believed in his name, he gave the right to become children of God—children born not of natural descent, nor of human decision or a husband's will, but born of God (Jn 1:12–13).

If you're not a Christian—if you don't genuinely know God—why not put this book down and surrender now to Jesus? Do you have eternal life? Will you go to heaven when you die? Are you enjoying the life of heaven now? Are you living under 'new management'—the lordship of Jesus? If you're not, why not? If you say, 'I don't know—I'm not too sure', that is a good indication that you're not a Christian. If you say to me, 'Bill, are you married?', I won't respond, 'I don't know, maybe, I think so.' I will say, *'Yes.'* You see, you're either married or not. You are either a Christian or you're not. Settle the issue. 'He who has the Son has life; he who does not have the Son of God does not have life' (1 Jn 5:12). You're either dead or alive. No Jesus—no life. Know Jesus—know life!

You can enjoy conversational prayer with the Lord and Creator of the universe when you become his child. You can live in the good of that worship song: 'I'm accepted, I'm forgiven, I am Fathered by the true and living God. I am accepted. No condemnation! I am loved by the true and living God.'

Fred Lemon was a hard-nut criminal transformed by the love of Jesus. He's into conversational prayer. He was at a prayer meeting. 'Hello, Lord, it's me again,' was the opener. He concluded with, 'I need a shave. I'll see you later.' With that, I understand that he made his exit from the early morning Bible week prayer meeting!

Fred was not being flippant. He was being himself, enjoying Daddy dialogue.

In one of their magazines, the National Secular Society states, 'Nobody is listening: Christians who actually believe in the power of prayer are an odd lot. For the more they bow the head, bend the knee and grovel to their God, the worse he treats them.' They go on to write of '...this sado-masochistic relationship between the Almighty and his sycophantic supplicants.'

The NSS, perhaps not surprisingly, have failed to grasp what prayer involves. We approach a loving Father with boldness. We come to speak to heavenly Dad. We don't need to grovel about in the dust. We are accepted by Father God and on that basis can enjoy praying to him.

3

Danger: High Voltage

Heroes. We all have them. Rock stars, film stars, foot-ballers. I was visiting the home of my hero. Loved by those in the three-decade-plus club, and known to all Wacaday wide-awakers. With a voice like a demonised Donald Duck, and the ability to leap out of the water, somersault and move backwards on the water on his tail. I was at Miami Seaquarium, the home of Flipper, the dolphin.

It's quite an impressive place. I visited the spot where many of the outdoor shots were filmed, saw the 'home' of Bud and Sandy and their jetty—even sat in the director's chair. However, Flipper is not the sole resident of the Miami Seaquarium. There are slimy sea elephants and performing seals. There is a huge killer whale which delights in leaping out of the water and belly-flopping back down in his pool, soaking the first three rows of spectators. And then there are the sharks.

The sharks have their very own pool. Not surprising, eh? It is moat shaped, and they move around the pool occasionally looking heavenward for lunch. Regular as clockwork, packed lunch glides out of reach above them— the monorail! From the monorail, you get a great pan-oramic view of the Seaquarium, and part of your journey takes you over the shark-infested moat.

The day I was there the monorail lurched to a halt—right over the shark pool. As you can imagine, the occupants of the vehicle were none too pleased. I can think of a lot of places I'd rather be on a hot Florida day than dangling over some peckish sharks. The perspiring passengers were getting slowly cooked in their portable greenhouse as the sunshine sizzled through the glass. Naturally no one was keen on opening the doors. The air conditioning seemed to be on the blink. A crowd gathered to watch the drama unfold. The monorail occupants finally got back to the ground—very vocal about their unplanned stop!

Many Christians suffer from the same problem: power failure. God's plan is for you to be a dangerous high voltage Christian. However, many Christians are like that Seaquarium monorail car: static, powerless, going nowhere fast. God's plan is for a people in love with Jesus experiencing the flow of the power of God in their lives. What revivalist Charles Finney said many years ago holds true today: 'The supreme need today is power from on high.'

In this chapter we will look at the ministry of the Holy Spirit in our praying. We'll find out how he helps and see how we can experience the supernatural power of the Holy Spirit in our praying. We need to heed Samuel Chadwick's words: 'We are never really men (or women!) of prayer in the best sense until we are filled with the Holy Spirit.'

In Zechariah 12:10 the Holy Spirit is described as the Spirit of prayer. Being filled with the Holy Spirit should therefore impact our praying!

Jesus promises the remedy for power failure in our living and praying. 'But you will receive power when the Holy Spirit comes on you' (Acts 1:8). Paul orders us, 'Be filled with the Spirit' (Eph 5:18). This is the secret of a high voltage prayer life—to invite Jesus to fill us and flood us with his Spirit.

'Prayer itself is an art which only the Holy Spirit can teach us. He is the giver of all prayer.' So stated Charles Spurgeon.

R. A. Torrey was an evangelist who impacted cities and nations through his dynamic ministry. He recognised how vital the work of the Holy Spirit is in our praying. He said, '...the whole secret of prayer is found in these three words: *in the Spirit*. It is prayer which God the Holy Spirit inspires that God the Father answers.'

God wants high voltage Christians who have tapped into heaven's power supply. 'The supreme need of today is power from on high.' That is the will of God for you. God does not want you to be a spiritual paralytic. He wants you to enjoy the supernatural power of the Holy Spirit in your life. God does not want you immobilised like that monorail in Miami—cut off from the power supply.

You don't need me to tell you how dangerous dangling above a shark pool is. The consequences of power failure spelled danger for the monorail occupants. The apostle Paul wrote to a group of believers in Ephesus. We have one of his prayers in print in Ephesians 3:14–21. Paul prays out of a deep desire that these Christians avoid the pitfalls and paralysis of power failure and that they live as high voltage Christians (Eph 3:19–20).

Paul recognised that the Christians in Ephesus were in a dangerous environment—a hotbed of occultism, immorality and prostitution. Look at Acts 19 where a riot was instigated because people were duped by demons— people pursuing a false religion worshipping a false goddess. From first-hand experience, Paul knew Ephesus was a war zone—a spiritually hostile environment to follow Jesus.

This knowledge perhaps fuelled the urgency of his praying. 'For this reason I kneel before the Father...'

(Eph 3:14). Kneeling is a prayer posture that communicates urgency and seriousness in prayer. What was the content of Paul's prayer? 'I pray that out of his glorious riches he may strengthen you with power through his Spirit in your inner being...that you may be filled to the measure of all the fulness of God' (Eph 3:16,19). Paul was desperate. He loved these people. He knew that if they experienced power failure they would be immobilised in a danger zone. Paul not only prayed that the Ephesians believers lived in the fullness of the Spirit, he commanded it: '...be filled with the Spirit' (Eph 5:18)!

You need to be full of the Spirit of God. Are you filled with the Holy Spirit? This is a definite experience that God expects all his children to enter into and enjoy. Christians delight in putting labels on each other. The enthusiasm for this pursuit is well matched in another hobby, a great evangelical pastime called doctrinal pigeon holes— fun for the whole family of God. The sad result is that we can get hung up on what we *call* this experience Jesus wants us to step into, and we can miss out on the real thing.

You might call the experience that Jesus promises:

The baptism with the Holy Spirit	Acts 1:5
The gift of the Holy Spirit	Acts 2:38, 10:45
Being filled with the Spirit	Acts 2:4
The promise of the Father	Acts 1:4, 2:39
Being endued with power from on high	Luke 24:49

The big question is not how theologically tidy your label is. The issue is, 'Did you receive the Holy Spirit when you believed?' (Acts 19:2).

A. W. Tozer, in *Man: The Dwelling Place of God*, hit the nail on the head: 'No one in the Scriptures or Christian biography was ever filled with the Spirit who did not know he had been, and nowhere was anyone filled who did not know when and no one was ever filled gradually.'

Now that Tozer has made things plain, have *you* been baptised in the Holy Spirit? Jesus is the baptiser. He wants to suffuse you, immerse you, drench you with his Spirit.

What a radical high voltage difference the Spirit coming upon the 120 made on the Day of Pentecost (Acts 2). Scared stiff Simon was transformed from the wimp who denied Jesus when a little girl challenged him, to a fearless preacher energised by supernatural boldness. The fullness of the Spirit changed Peter from a man of paste and flour to a man of faith and power. People sometimes fall into the trap of viewing Pentecost as a one-off event. In a sense it was. The church was born. You can't repeat that. But that experience of the Spirit's power that the 120 received from Jesus was repeated again and again throughout the Book of Acts.

Jesus openly invites you to let him fill you with his Spirit. You can have a personal Pentecost. It's for you! The promise is for you and your children and for all who are far off—for all whom the Lord our God will call (Acts 2:39).

I'm not going to labour the point any further. Why not shut the book, shut yourself in with Jesus, and invite him to fill you to overflowing with Holy Spirit streams of living water? As that great Scottish theologian, James Denney, reminded us, 'Pentecost was won for us at Calvary.' Jesus did not die for you so that you could live an anaemic, dry, powerless existence as a Christian. The Holy Spirit came upon Jesus not just to empower his ministry, but also that through Jesus, crucified and risen, the Holy Spirit may be given to all flesh. You don't have to run on empty. A car can't do that; neither can you. Power from on high—is that your experience, or are you cut off from the power supply? Ask Father God and you'll receive (Lk 11:13).

The Holy Spirit wants to empower and energise our praying. Some translations call him the Helper. He wants to help us in our praying.

I had the privilege of hearing the late preacher Alan Redpath at a Youth For Christ staff retreat. He spent a day with us and said many wonderful, helpful and probing things. During the course of his time with us he said, 'What does God expect of you? Nothing but failure! But he has given us the Holy Spirit so that we need not fail. The Christian life is not self-improvement, but Christ-replacement.'

There's a lot of good news locked in Alan Redpath's words. God has a realistic view of us. He does not dismiss us because of our weaknesses or failures. The Holy Spirit wants to help us in our problems and as we struggle to pray (Rom 8:27). When it comes to prayer it's very easy to feel absolutely useless. If a preacher wants to make his congregation squirm, all he has to do is preach on prayerlessness. He towers above us all in the security of his pulpit, six feet above contradiction. He fires his exocet: 'How long have you spent in prayer today? How much time have you spent on your knees this week, people?' (You are no longer a human being, you are a 'people'!)

There's a danger that youth leaders and preachers just drop a guilt bomb on us rather than actually propelling us into the prayer adventure.

There's release in knowing what God expects of us, in prayer. Nothing but failure! Jesus informs us, 'Apart from me you can do nothing' (Jn 15:5). Here's good news—he has given us the Holy Spirit so that we need not be failures when it comes to prayer.

You need to get hold of the principle Alan Redpath communicated to the Youth for Christ bods who assembled for staff retreat. The Christian life is not self-improvement—it is Christ-replacement. It is Jesus living his life in and through you by his Spirit. 'Christ in you, the hope of glory,' as the Bible puts it (Col 1:27).

The Holy Spirit reproduces the life of Jesus in us. That's why real followers of Jesus look like their leader. The Holy Spirit makes this happen (2 Cor 3:18). When we talk about the fruit of the Spirit and the gifts of the Spirit we're talking about the character and the conduct of Jesus. We're talking about the Holy Spirit doing his job and making you into a mini Jesus! The fruit and the gifts are the life and power and beauty of Jesus being activated in your life by the Spirit of God who has come to make your life his home.

Brilliant, but how does this affect me as I struggle to get my prayer life together?

Catch this. What Jesus has done and is doing *for* us— the Holy Spirit does *in* us. Jesus is praying for us. Right now, as you scan the words on this page, Jesus is praying for you! The Bible tells us he is our Great High Priest and that 'He always lives to intercede for [us]' (Heb 7:25). In other words, non-stop, night and day, Jesus prays for you. He sits at the Father's right hand and represents you before the Father. It's mind-blowing! There is a man in heaven—the Lord Jesus—praying for you. But, there's more!

While Jesus prays for you, the Holy Spirit prays in you and through you. The Holy Spirit is the indwelling intercessor (see Romans 8:26–27).

The heavenly Helper wants to energise and empower and direct your praying. The Bible refers to the Spirit of God as 'the Spirit of grace and supplication' or the Spirit of prayer (Zech 12:10).

Well, how does the Helper help us?

Some translations refer to the Holy Spirit as the Comforter. I don't know about you, but for me 'Comforter' conjures up certain images: making cups of tea for upset little grannies, mopping beads of perspiration from tired brows, producing Kleenex boxes and dabbing teary eyes, and so on. However, these tender grandfatherly images do not tie in with what comfort means. A clearer understanding of the Holy Spirit as Comforter is found in the Bayeux tapestry. Word meanings have changed since the seventeenth century. Readers of the King Jimbo Bible please note!

The Bayeux tapestry depicts King William's victory at the Battle of Hastings. One caption reads, 'King William comforteth his soldiers.' What does that section on the tapestry depict? King William planting kisses on his battle-weary troops? The king hugging his dear little soldiers and pouring isotonic Lucozade down their throats to revitalise their tired bodies? *No*. The caption refers to a tapestry section where a reluctant warrior is being encouraged to get into the thick of things by means of a dirty great spear applied to his rear end.

In the same way, the Spirit of God, as Comforter, mobilises us into the thick of the action. He prods and prompts us to be pray-ers.

Confident and clean (and nothing to do with Colgate toothpaste, thank you very much!)

It is the Holy Spirit who assures us that Father God has accepted us. Paul tells us, 'The Spirit himself testifies with our spirit that we are God's children' (Rom 8:16). The Living Bible's paraphrase throws helpful light on this truth: 'For his Holy Spirit speaks to us deep in our hearts, and tells us that we really are God's children.' This fuels our prayers with confidence. God has accepted us; he loves us. His love towards us never lets up, never dims, never weakens, and it is completely unconditional. Father loves us with an everlasting, never failing love. We are his own dear children. We have been adopted into God's family. We have 'received the Spirit of sonship' and it is the Spirit of God who enables us to cry, 'Abba, Father' (take a look at Romans 8:15). That little word 'Abba' is Aramaic for 'Daddy'. This expresses the intimacy that we've been drawn into. We know we have access to God in prayer because the Holy Spirit burns the reality into our hearts that God is our Father.

'We know that we live in him and he in us, because he has given us of his Spirit' (1 Jn 4:13). 'And this is how we know that he lives in us: We know it by the Spirit he gave us' (1 Jn 3:24).

H. G. Wells told the story of a prominent man who was so stressed out and under pressure that he was on the road to having a mental and emotional cave-in. He was told by his doctor that the only remedy for his condition was the peace that flows out of a relationship with God. The man, however, did not show much enthusiasm for this spiritual medicine offered him.

'What! To think of that, up there, having fellowship with me! I would as soon think of cooling my throat with the Milky Way or shaking hands with the stars.'

However, if you're a Christian you know that God is not 'that up there'. He is not a distant deity tucked away in some remote corner of a galaxy. If you are a Christian, God is your Father. The Holy Spirit is the One who enables you to live in the good of that glorious fact.

It was the Holy Spirit who showed you your need of Jesus. He convicted you of your rebellion and wrong-doing before God. He showed you your need of forgiveness and rescue. The Holy Spirit loves to put the spotlight on Jesus and the spotlight on sinners' sins so that we run to the Saviour. However, the Spirit's floodlighting operations do not draw to a close when we became Christians. He continues to put the spotlight on areas of our lives that need to be put right before God. Sin leads to communication breakdown. The Holy Spirit shows us areas in our lives that displease God in order that we can experience forgiveness and cleansing and enjoy open lines of communication with the Father.

Because of the Holy Spirit's activity in your life, you don't have to live paralysed by doubt and fear. God proved his love for you unmistakably on the cross of Jesus. By his Spirit God pours his love into our hearts (Rom 5:5). This is not some theological abstraction to agree with, but a living experience to be enjoyed. The overshadowing reality of basking in God's love fuels our praying with confidence. The reality of the love of God in our hearts brings us to the place where we recognise we're not in the business of extracting blessing from an unwilling God. We are coming to One who loves us with an everlasting love. Romans 8:31b–32 tells us, 'If God is for us, who can be against us? He who did not spare his own Son, but gave him up for us all—how will he not also, along with him, graciously give us all things?'

> Because you are sons, God sent the Spirit of his Son into our hearts, the Spirit who calls out, 'Abba, Father.' So you are no longer a slave, but a son; and since you are a son, God has made you also an heir (Gal 4:6–7).

Good news! The heavenly Helper helps the helpless pray-er

The Bible tells us, '. . . the Spirit helps us in our weakness. We do not know what we ought to pray for, but the Spirit himself intercedes for us with groans that words cannot express. And he who searches our hearts knows the mind of the Spirit, because the Spirit intercedes for the saints in accordance with God's will' (Rom 8:26–27).

Sometimes we are totally ignorant of what to pray for. We find ourselves in the position where our perception is fuzzy and we just can't seem to get a handle on God's agenda for the situation. As a result we just don't know what to target in prayer. If you've faced the puzzling

dilemma of saying, 'What is God's will in these circum-
stances? What should I be praying for?—good news! The
Holy Spirit comes to our rescue. '...the Spirit helps us in
our weakness.' The Greek word which is translated 'helps'
means 'take in hand'. It is actually made up of three
words. So what's being communicated here?

Suppose you're out in the garden struggling with a
piece of equipment—or perhaps a huge boulder—that is
actually too heavy for you to cope with. Your next-door
neighbour, muscles rippling, arrives on the scene. She
grabs hold of the other end of the object that is causing
you such grief. What you could not alone do is accomplished by a partnership. You move the boulder together
without mutilating your garden gnome. Together you
shifted the boulder. This is how Paul describes the Spirit
of God coming to our rescue.

The same verb is used in Luke 10:40. Mary enjoys
fellowship with Jesus in the living room. Meanwhile, in
the kitchen, Martha stomps around like a rhinoceros with
hobnail boots on. There's a mountain of grotty crockery.
There are pots violently hissing on the cooker. There is a
huge cake in the oven. There are spuds to be peeled and a
salad to be prepared. An ill-tempered coffee pot spits
furiously away near the window sill. The kitchen has
turned into a sauna. The noise inside is as reassuring as
being lullabied with a pneumatic drill. Martha is not
singing, 'Bless the Lord, O my soul' at this point. She is
fuming, 'Where is that sister of mine?'

She remembers that Mary is with Jesus. She appeals to
the Lord, 'Tell her to *help* me! Tell Mary to get in here and
give me a hand, Lord.'

This is how the Spirit helps us. He gets 'in there to give
us a hand'. He helps us by taking hold of our burdens so
that we can pray in line with God's will. He guides our
praying because he knows the mind of the Lord and the
Father 'who searches our hearts [and] knows the mind of

54

the Spirit' (Rom 8:27). There's complete and perfect understanding between Father and Holy Spirit. The Holy Spirit comes to us in our confusion and struggles, and he grasps the situation for us and with us. He prays in us and through us to the Father. This praying is wordless—a silent burden of the heart communicated to the Father by the Spirit; his 'groans that words cannot express'. Again, this reinforces the fact that prayer is a matter of the heart, not of eloquence. Sometimes we are at a loss for words— we cannot adequately express what we want to say. We aren't even sure what we should be saying. The Holy Spirit within you prays on your behalf.

Prayer language

We've discovered that the Holy Spirit can help us pray when we are at a loss for words. He prays through us. However, he can help you in another way. The Spirit of God can give you a prayer language. You are enabled by the Spirit to pray to God in a language that you have never learned. Yes, I'm talking about 'tongues'.

If you read the Book of Acts you'll discover some interesting things that happened to people when the Spirit of God came upon them. In some of these instances, Dr Luke informs us that those who received the Spirit spoke in tongues. At the outpouring on Pentecost Day we are told, 'All of them were filled with the Holy Spirit and began to speak in other tongues as the Spirit enabled them' (Acts 2:4). We are told that the Jewish believers who accompanied Peter to a house meeting knew the Holy Spirit had come upon the Gentiles because '...they heard them speaking in tongues and praising God' (see Acts 10:45–47). When Paul placed his hands on some Ephesian disciples '...the Holy Spirit came on them, and they spoke in tongues and prophesied' (Acts 19:6).

Further on in the New Testament, Paul gave some

guidelines to believers in the church at Corinth about the use of tongues in public and in private. The Corinthian Christians were abusing the gift of tongues. Paul's remedy for abuse of spiritual gifts was to encourage proper use. You will find Paul's instructions very helpful. A study of 1 Corinthians 12—14 will be profitable for gaining an understanding of what 'tongues' is all about.

The term 'tongues' might seem a bit mysterious to you. The word means 'languages', nothing more. But it is a supernatural gift of the Holy Spirit. By using your prayer language, your spirit communicates directly with God, without your mind being used in the process, by an unlearned language given to you by the Holy Spirit.

Paul said when he prayed in tongues that this is what happened: 'If I pray in a tongue my spirit prays but my mind is unfruitful' (1 Cor 14:14). This does not mean that Paul's brain went on strike, and while he prayed in tongues he became a heavenly zombie. Paul was saying that his mind was unproductive.

At this point, some of our rationalist brothers and sisters get nervous. The Living Bible is helpful here: 'For if I pray in tongues, my spirit is praying but I don't know what I am saying' (1 Cor 14:14).

So, what's the use of praying if I don't know what I'm saying? Your mind can act as a filter or a censor which inhibits your praying. You are bypassing the censoring mechanism. You are talking to God, uttering mysteries by the Holy Spirit (1 Cor 14:2). When you pray in tongues your spirit is doing the praying. By the operation of this gift you can rise above the inadequacy of your mother tongue. You can move beyond the limits of your language and your understanding.

Praying in tongues is a means of building yourself up spiritually (1 Cor 14:4). This can be done while driving the car or mowing the lawn. If you pray in English you've got to keep your mind on the business of prayer. This is not the case when your prayer language is in operation. Paul Yonggi Cho says he prays in tongues while he reads his Bible!

In her superb book, *Chasing the Dragon*, Jackie Pullinger relates the story of how one woman's spiritual life took off because as she worked her way through mounds of ironing, she spent the time praying in tongues. You will find that the use of this gift can have a similar building up effect in your life. Praying in tongues can be a source of spiritual refreshment to you (see Isaiah 28:11–12).

Tongues can be used as a heavenly love language with which to praise God (see Acts 2:11; 10:46).

Tongues is not only a means of enjoying intimacy with Father. It can be a tremendous aid to intercession. For one thing, you are enabled to pray for longer. If you are drawing to the end of what you can say in English, use your prayer language! You can bring a person or a situation before the Lord in your heart and pray out to God in the tongue he has given you.

4

Shut That Door

We hadn't been married all that long and we'd been given a gift to buy some furniture. Our little flat had not much cupboard space. The obvious item to buy was a cupboard. Did we buy a ready-just-to-place-in-the living room unit? Oh no! We bought one of those wonderful DIY kits. The amazing thing is that they look wonderful in the shop. They are supposed to be a doddle to put together.

The instructions never make much sense. If you follow them you cannot build your closet. There's always a strategic paragraph in the booklet missing. There are usually three screws that you cannot find. They should be in that little plastic bag that you had to tear open with your teeth. The three screws sit on a factory floor in Hong Kong. Small wonder your search through the carpet is futile. I reckon the supreme champion of *The Krypton Factor* would struggle with the demands that this project would place on his or her ingenuity. Professor Rubik, inventor of 'that cube' and other assorted puzzles, would surely come to grief. So, what chance did we have?

We were thrilled to have been given the money. We were thrilled to have purchased our very own cupboard with its fake teak top and yellow doors. When we took the thing home our joy very quickly evaporated. Even the very screws did not want to get into place. I abandoned the

screwdriver and drove those rebellious screws into position with a hammer.

Constructing our closet proved to be a source of great
frustration to Morag and me. Jesus assumed we would all
build prayer closets (see Matthew 6:6). For many of us the
idea is fine—maybe even exciting. But when it comes to
the construction of a prayer closet—a time when we shut
ourselves in with God—we struggle to get it together and
end up very frustrated. How can we put together a prayer
closet?

In this chapter I want to share with you some practical
ideas on cultivating time with God in your 'prayer closet'.

Get alone with God

In Matthew 6:5 Jesus gives us very helpful instruction on
the life of prayer. He warns us against seeing prayer as a
performance—a means of impressing the public (Mt 6:5).
Prayer involves baring our hearts before God. Jesus tells
us if we want to meet with Father, our praying should be a
private affair. Obviously, there is a place for corporate
public prayer, but here we are told: 'go into your room,
close the door'. Jesus informs us: 'your Father...sees what
is done in secret' (Mt 6:6).

There are two issues involved in Jesus' instruction.
Firstly, prayer is a heart issue. Prayer is not a decibel
issue—how loud we can shout to God. Prayer is not an
eloquence issue—how nice what I say to God sounds.
Prayer is not an aerobics issue. God is far more interested
in the posture of our hearts than the posture of our knees.
Jesus contrasts the true disciples of Jesus with 'the hypo-
crites'. Doubtless, Jesus was referring to the Pharisees.
Throughout the Sermon on the Mount, Jesus is concerned
with our motives and what goes on in the depths of our
hearts.

A 'hypocrite' was a performer, or an actor, or an orator.

In other words, someone good on the stage, in the spotlight. That's not what prayer's about.

Gerard Kelly, a British Youth For Christ staff worker,
puts it very well in his poem, 'The Games People Pray':

> Some pray like a BMW:
> Seven coats
> Of shine and shimmer
> Masking the hardness of steel,
> With an Anti-Emotion Warranty
> To guard against
> The least sign of trust.
>
> Some pray like a Porsche:
> Nought to victory
> In 6.7 seconds,
> Banking on the promises
> Of Pray-As-You-Earn prosperity.
>
> Jesus recommended
> Praying in the garage
> With the door shut,
> Engine and radio off,
> Praying when no-one is looking,
> Forgetting
> The traffic of the day.
> Meeting God
> In the quiet lay-by,
> Far from
> The Pray and Display.[11]

Secondly, Jesus says, 'Shut that door.' He wants us to
shut the clamour of life's busy distractions out. Get shut in
somewhere with God where you can enjoy undisturbed
prayer time. You can of course pray anywhere. You can
pray soaking in a hot bath or walking the dog. You can
talk to God riding the bus or pushing a trolley through the

supermarket. I often pray while I'm driving the car. Some
might say my driving's got a lot to do with it. But in the
car, sometimes it's just the Lord and I on a trip together. I
take the opportunity to sing to him, to pour out my heart
to him and to listen to him.

We can pray 'arrow prayers'. We can fire up prayers to
heaven like Nehemiah did. Nehemiah was a man of prayer
who could spend a lengthy period seeking the face of God
(Neh 1:4). He could pray prayers of theological depth and
understanding (Neh 1:5–11). In Nehemiah 2:4–5 he is in
conversation with the king. The king asks Nehemiah a
question and before our hero responds he shoots an arrow
prayer to heaven. That's a good practice to adopt. Recognise the fact that you can turn to God anywhere and any
time.

However, Jesus was recommending the practice of lock-
ing yourself in your prayer closet. Get away from everyone
and spend time with God, and nobody else but God.
Great—but how can you manage to get shut in with God?

When my wife, Morag, was a young Christian she
literally shut herself in a cupboard in her room. She had a
desk, a lamp and her Bible. Tucked away in her prayer
closet she would pray to the Father without getting interrupted.

A friend of mine put some carpet and a chair in a
garden shed. He would take his Bible and guitar in there
and spend time with God, alone. He would read the
Scriptures, sing to God and pray. Morag and Tim under-
stood the need to commune with God unhindered by
distractions.

How can you avoid screaming kids, the telephone (why
does the whole world stop for a telephone?) and the roar of
the television or radio? Why not get up before everyone
else kicks into gear? That was Jesus' game plan: 'Very
early in the morning, while it was still dark, Jesus got up,

left the house and went off to a solitary place, where he prayed' (Mk 1:35).

Do you get the picture? The disciples are still unconscious in bed. Jesus removes himself from potential distraction and heads for a quiet unoccupied area. Even then, we are told good old sensitive 'Simon and his companions went to look for him, and when they found him, they exclaimed: "Everyone is looking for you!" ' (Mk 1:36–37). A search party had been organised. Once the disciples discovered Jesus, his solitude with the Father was broken and demands were placed on him.

If you know that your home will be like a zoo with every cage unlocked by 7.30 am, you need to be praying before then! You need to have a game plan—decide how long you are going to spend with God. Make an appointment with Father and plan accordingly.

You might well ask, 'How long should I pray for?' There's a Chinese proverb that says, 'A journey of 1,000 miles begins with the first step.' Start with a realistic goal of time spent with God in prayer and move on from there. As I write this I am fighting a slow tortuous battle against the flab. If you met me right now you'd recognise I've got to lose weight. Hopefully, you'd be too polite to open our conversation with that observation. The point is, I'm not an athlete. I'm in no condition to run a twenty-six mile marathon today. Such a prospect might never happen. If I am to become a marathon man it would take time and discipline. I would have to break myself in gently. I wouldn't start with twenty-six, or even a ten mile run. A more realistic training programme might begin with a jog round the housing estate.

If you are not praying at all in a regular way at this moment you will find it difficult to sustain two hours in prayer. Agreed? Why not start with fifteen or twenty minutes, or even ten minutes and build on that. Soon you will discover that the time you spend praying will grow.

Once you've decided how long you plan to spend with God, act accordingly. You may decide that 5.30 in the morning is a great time to get alone with God. The house is quiet—not a creature is stirring, not even a mouse! Those conditions provide an ideal environment to pour out your heart to God. However, if you come in and watch the late film, have some supper, snatch some nocturnal video viewing and crawl into bed at 1.45 am you will have difficulty stirring at 5.30 am. Try it and see!

Alan Redpath said that Christians need to experience blanket victory. He meant we need to get out from underneath them! That battle is won or lost the night before. You can't burn the candle at both ends! If you want to have an early bird appointment with God, you can't be an owl at night.

You need to set a time and a place for prayer and stick to it. You might not have a garden shed to shut yourself in with God, but appoint a place for your praying, set a time and honour your appointment with God. There needs to be a measure of discipline in our lives if we are going to take the call to prayer seriously. American pastor, Larry Lea, says, 'Prayer is a discipline before it is a delight.'

Is the morning special?

I've made reference to an early to bed, early to rise commitment to prayer. The psalmist said, 'In the morning, O Lord, you hear my voice; in the morning I lay my requests before you and wait in expectation' (Ps 5:3).

D. L. Moody knew that if we don't *make* time to pray we will not *take* time to pray. He saw the value of making prayer the first appointment in the day:

We ought to see the face of God every morning before we see the face of man. If you have so much business to attend to that you have not time to pray, depend upon it that you have more business on hand than God ever intended.

Jesus sought his Father in prayer before dawn (Mk 1:35). Many great men and women of God who impacted history were people who faced God before they faced the day. The Cambridge Seven from late last century were a missionary force who punched holes in the kingdom of darkness. Their missionary fruit and missionary call can be traced back to a commitment they made. They decided to observe the 'morning watch'. In other words, they committed themselves to meet with God at the start of each day.

The little episode in the life of Jesus we've referred to in Mark 1 shows the importance of meeting God before we meet the day. The disciples barge in on Jesus and cut across his praying with the announcement, 'Everyone is looking for you!' (Mk 1:36). In other words: 'You're needed, Jesus. Quick, you need to get a move on, Lord.'

Jesus is informed, 'The people over here need you.' He responds, 'Let us go somewhere else' (Mk 1:37). Jesus let heaven's priorities dominate his timetable, not a bunch of excitable fishermen waving filofaxes. In the place of prayer Jesus aligned himself with the perfect will of his Father. I am convinced the reason he responded the way he did was because he had received guidance in prayer. He met with his Father before he met the demands of the day. Elsewhere, Jesus could say, '...the Son...can do only what he sees his Father doing, because whatever the Father does the Son also does' (Jn 5:19). Jesus' ministry and activity flowed out of his relationship with his Father. This relationship was cultivated by prayer.

Alan Redpath warned us, 'Beware the barrenness of a busy life.' We need to take our cue from Jesus. If we don't build time for prayer into our lives it will not magically slot into our routine. The temptation is to feel that we are too busy. Martin Luther, the hero of the Reformation, said, 'Work, work and more work from early until late. In fact I have so much to do that I shall spend the first three hours in prayer.'

Such a chunk of prayer might intimidate you. Don't let it. Apply the principle: you're never too busy to pray. If you are—you're too busy.

Take practical measures to ensure you pray. Early to bed makes early to rise more likely to happen. I found setting two alarms a helpful ploy in getting up. One clock in the bedroom—the other in the hall or bathroom. We're all prone to killing a bedside alarm clock. Put the bedroom clock as far away from your bed as possible. This means you'll need to move to turn it off! Similarly, an alarm clock in the hall will not bless your family...if it goes off! An alarm clock in the echo chamber of the bathroom will not win you most wonderful member of the household prize...if it goes off. Your mission is to defuse the alarm clock situated within earshot of your mum, dad, brother, sister, granny or poodle.

After the alarm clock aerobics you may be ready to shut the door of your prayer closet behind you. On the other hand, cold water on the outside and caffeine on the inside may be the order of the day. Now head for your appointed meeting place with God—the kitchen, dining room or in your own room.

A pattern and a tool kit

To build prayer into the fabric of your life, it helps to designate a place and a time with God. You might find it helpful to think about how you will spend your praying time. Come equipped to meet with God. Take your Bible. You will discover that the word of God will come alive out of prayer. The word of God keeps you in line and on track with your praying. You will find it helpful to read some chunks from the Bible before you start to pray. The word of God tunes your ears and heart into God's wavelength and guards you against deception. Reading the Bible before you pray gives God the opportunity to speak to you before you speak to him. George Muller has been called an 'apostle of faith'. He saw extraordinary answers to prayer. His practice was to read the Bible before he prayed. Muller would meditate on the word and chew it over and over. When God had spoken to him through the word, Muller would then pray. Have your Bible handy while you pray. That way you can consult it when praying.

Keep a notebook—that way you can record the voice of God. When God speaks to you, write it down. Put your prayer issues down on paper. You can record your prayer requests and put the date of entry down. Then you can rejoice in writing when and how God answered. You might want to devote a page of your notebook to a single prayer issue. You might want to keep a prayer file. You can get a cardboard wallet or a folder quite cheaply. Fill it with photos of missionaries you pray for. Put in prayer letters or prayer reports from churches, organisations and individuals you are praying for. If you are praying for political or international issues, put relevant newspaper cuttings in your file. Spread your stuff out and then pray for those folks you've put in your file. Update your file regularly so that you can pray intelligently in line with current needs.

You will need a prayer outline or pattern to follow. When I advocate a prayer system I'm not promoting a straightjacket, simply a framework to help you pray.

When the disciples came to Jesus requesting, 'Lord teach us to pray', Jesus' response was to offer them (and us) a pattern or framework for prayer. There is nothing unspiritual about having a structured prayer time. Jesus encouraged the disciples to use a system. You will find a prayer outline very helpful.

If you've ever been to a Change the Word School of Prayer you will have been introduced to a prayer system.

'The school' is run by World Literature Crusade and is an excellent motivation to pray with very helpful teaching. Those who attend the school are encouraged to think about spending an hour a day in prayer. CWSOP divides the hour into twelve five minute segments. Each segment is devoted to an aspect of prayer like praise or confession or intercession.

I don't know who invented the ACTS prayer scheme. This scheme encourages us to think about the ingredients of our prayers. ACTS stands for Adoration, Confession, Thanksgiving and Supplication. Supplication means making requests to God—for yourself and for others.

I don't always use it, but I have found using the Lord's Prayer as a prayer structure to be revolutionary. The Lord's Prayer was never meant to be mumbled en masse at morning school assemblies. It was not designed to be just a corporate recitation in Sunday morning worship. It is a device to help you pray. Break it down into chunks and use it as your approach to God. Jesus tells us 'this is how you should pray'.

1. 'Our Father in heaven, hallowed be your name.'

At the start of your prayer time celebrate your relationship with God. Spend time praising God that he is your Father, and you're his child. Start your time of prayer by focusing on the fatherhood of God. Reflect on his characteristics. Praise him for who he is. Give thanks that you're a child of the Father, because of Jesus. Spend time praising God for Jesus. Worship him because of his perfect life, atoning death, resurrection and endless life. You might want to sing songs that express your love for the Father and your gratitude to Jesus. The Father has accepted us because of what Jesus has done for us.

When we pray 'Our Father' we focus on God, not on ourselves. Jesus is the way to the Father (Jn 14:6). Spend time thanking Jesus that he has introduced us to his

Father. Jesus' blood guarantees us access to Father's heart. Meditate on what Jesus' death and resurrection has made possible and turn your meditation into thanksgiving. You have the right to call God Father!

'Hallowed be your name' is an invitation to worship. To hallow God's name means to reverence his name. We are praying that God's name be honoured and kept holy. Here is a reminder that we should not be flippant in God's presence or take his name lightly.

Here, you might find it useful to use the name of God as stepping stones for praise, or launch pads for praying your needs and the needs of others.

He is Jehovah Tsidkenu—the Lord our righteousness. Take the opportunity to thank God that he does not hold our sin against us. Our account has been credited with the perfect righteousness of Jesus. We have been put right with the righteous and holy God. 'God made him who had no sin to become sin for us, so that in him we might become the righteousness of God' (2 Cor 5:21).

God is Jehovah M'Kaddesh—the Lord who sanctifies. In other words, the Lord who makes us holy. Thank God that he is committed to making us like Jesus. You might want to bring areas of your life that need refining to him at this time.

These names of God correspond to the fact that he has dealt with our sin. Jesus has taken the penalty for our sin and broken the enslaving power of sin. God is our righteousness. He has righteous-ified us, or justified us. In his eyes it is just as if I'd never sinned. I've been acquitted. These are things we can praise God for with hearts filled with thanks.

He is Jehovah Shalom—the Lord is my peace. We can thank God that 'we have peace with God through our Lord Jesus Christ' (Rom 5:1). Jesus put his supernatural peace in our hearts—a peace that the world can't rob us of (Jn 14:27). The Bible declares, 'You will keep in perfect peace him whose mind is steadfast because he trusts in you' (Is 26:3). At this point don't just thank God for his peace; pray his peace into peoples' lives and pray for the peace of the kingdom to invade places like Belfast and Beirut.

Shalom means a lot more than peace of mind. It means harmony, integration and wholeness. Jesus is our peace. The word 'Shalom' appears in the Old Testament over 350 times, and Jesus is the fulfilment of all the Old Testament points to when it speaks of Shalom. He is the Prince of Peace. His kingdom means justice, peace and joy in the Holy Spirit. At this point in our praying we can pray for reconciliation to take place where there is brokenness, alienation and hatred and fear (see Ephesians 2:14–17).

We pray to Jehovah Shammah. The Lord is there, the Lord is present, is what this name means. Take time to thank God that he is with you, his hand is upon you. God promises you his presence. You can be filled with the living God. Here, thank God for the Holy Spirit and his ministry in your life. Invite God to fill you with his Holy Spirit. Pray for others to experience the fullness of the Spirit and the reality of the presence of God.

Jehovah Rophe—the Lord is my healer. Here take time to pray for those who need the healing touch of Jesus.

Jehovah Jireh—the Lord is my provider. Praise God that he is committed to meeting your needs. He will release into your life all you need to execute his will in your life. We pray to Jehovah Nissi—the Lord is our banner of victory. He is with us in our battles. The Lord is our security in adversity.

Similarly, you can use other names of God in your prayer. The names of God reveal something of his character. These names are fuel for praise and thanksgiving and adoration. The names of God give us confidence in our praying. They reveal what God is like and what he is committed to.

The Bible refers to 'Our Father' as Jehovah Rohi—the Lord is my shepherd. He is our security and our protection.

When we pray we pray to Jehovah Sabaoth—'The Lord of hosts, the King of glory.' He is Jehovah Elyon, 'The Lord most high.' While we are enabled to cry 'Abba! Daddy in heaven! I love you', we need to remember that we are praying to the eternal King of the universe. We are in the presence of royalty, the King of kings. We should pray accordingly with reverence in our hearts.

2. 'Come, kingdom of God'

Jesus told us to pray: 'Come, your kingdom! Be done your will here on the earth as it is in heaven.'

Jesus has instructed us to pray 'down with heaven'! Here he invites us to bring heaven and earth closer together by our praying. We are to pray in the form of royal commands. Come, kingdom of God! Be done will of God! Here we are giving God unlimited right to step into our lives, our church, our family, our society. We invite God to establish his kingdom in our lives, the lives of our friends and family, our church, our school, our country. As we pray for individuals, pray that the righteousness/justice of God is established in their lives. Pray that King Jesus establishes his reign in their lives. Pray that he invades our lives and land at every level.

Here pray for your friends who are not yet Christians. Pray that they might surrender to King Jesus. Spend time praying for non-Christian friends and members of your family. Pray for Christian leaders. Don't get introspective. Yes, pray for God's kingdom to break into your life in newer and deeper ways. But pray beyond yourself and your little circle. Pray that where there is injustice God's rule would break in. 'But let justice roll on like a river, righteousness like a never-failing stream!' (Amos 5:24). Perhaps you could get on your knees with the newspaper and pray God's kingdom into national and international issues.

3. 'Give us this day our daily bread'

Jesus not only instructs us to pray for the extension of God's kingdom, he invites us to bring our own personal needs to God. A loving Father who is interested in every detail of our lives. Here we can bring our own spiritual and physical needs to God. This is where the notebook comes in handy. If we record people's needs as we become aware of them, we have an up-to-date record of prayer requests.

4. 'Forgive us our debts as we forgive our debtors'

Here we can receive forgiveness for ourselves. Also, before God, we forgive and release anyone who has wronged us and pray that they might experience forgiveness. Pray God's best into them.

5. 'Lead us not into temptation but deliver us from evil'

During this part of the Lord's Prayer you might find it useful to pray on the armour of God (Eph 6). Pick up your weapons and pray protection upon yourself and others.

At the conclusion return to praise, declaring to God: 'Yours is the kingdom and the power and the glory for ever.'

Mind your language

The name of the Lord is a 'strong tower', Scripture says— not a comma! I would get just a wee bit frustrated if you and I went for a coffee and you said, 'Bill, it's just been such a day, Bill. Bill, the cat got stuck up a tree, Bill. And Bill, the firemen came, Bill, and Bill, they came and climbed up the tree, Bill, and Bill...' Get the idea? Don't use God as a device to punctuate your praying.

I know God understands extinct languages but you don't have to remind him of them. There's nothing particularly holy about thee-ing and thou-ing. Back to the coffee shop. How would you feel if I leaned across the table and said, 'O thou great and wonderful friend of mine, thou precious loving companion. Thou knowest that I am a man of great thirst. I beseech thee, would thou bestowest upon me out of the depths of thy great kindness and affection toward me another cup of coffee'?

Some folk switch voices and accents to pray and change their language. God wants us to be ourselves. We do not get closer to heaven by speaking Zionese or addressing God in seventeenth-century English. We've all heard folk pray with the voice of an aristocrat with worms. We meet up with them later and they have reverted to 'normal'. There is no such thing as a 'spiritual' voice.

Be yourself when you pray. We approach God with love and reverence, so Big Buddy in the sky praying is out of order. But you can be honest with God. Don't put on phony voices, and don't put on phony emotions or masks when you pray. Bring him your joy or your grief. If you're angry or frustrated, let him know. He knows already, and God is big enough to deal with your ups and downs. Read the Psalms—there you see honesty in prayer to God. Take your cue from the Psalms.

Keeping on track

I've already mentioned the fact that we can get distracted and interrupted in prayer. We need to plan accordingly. I'm convinced that one of the reasons Jesus spent whole nights in prayer and got up very early to pray was he wanted to enjoy unbroken fellowship and communion with his Father. Jesus' prayer life was not a haphazard activity.

Even when we achieve solitude we can struggle to stay

on track in prayer. Even if the whole family is absent or asleep we can battle with other distractions. Even in tranquil surroundings we can struggle to keep focused. How do you deal with wandering thoughts? What happens when your brain goes off at a tangent? What do you do when drowsiness begins to creep over you?

You will find praying out loud a helpful way to deal with distractions. You don't have to sit or kneel in one spot when you pray. Move around. Pacing about in your room, walking and talking, will help combat tiredness's attempts to overcome you. If you are distracted by your environment, closing your eyes might help. Although, moving around with your eyes closed is not recommended! If you are feeling tired at night, closing your eyes could have quite an effect on your prayer life—but you will feel very refreshed when you wake up the next day! There is nothing particularly holy or special about closing your eyes when you pray. Jesus probably didn't pray with his eyes shut (see John 17:1).

You might find earplugs or headphones are useful if things are noisy in your surroundings.

On the move

You don't have to remain static when you pray. When you are praying for God's kingdom to come in your life and when you are surrendering to his perfect will, you might want to lie prostrate on the floor. When you are praising God, you might want to stand with your hands lifted heavenwards. When you confess your sins and ask God for cleansing and forgiveness, you might want to kneel before him.

When you pray for your area and the needs of your locality and the people who live there, why not take to the streets? Let your prayer agenda be shaped by what you see as you walk through your neighbourhood and town. For example, as you pass the Burger King, pray that the kids who hang about outside might get saved. As you walk past the schools, pray for the staff and students. As you pass church buildings, pray for the leadership and the people who gather there. In Chapter 6, Being a Bridge, we will look more closely at praying for others. We'll look at the ministry of the intercessor and an intercessory agenda.

In closing, can I urge you to make use of some excellent prayer resources. Trevor Gregory of BYFC, and the Evangelical Alliance's Youth Prayer Co-ordinator, has pioneered the Warrior tape.[12] It is 'the most up to date, hip-hop guide to real effective prayer'. It's a prayer framework on audio cassette. In a fast moving action-packed presentation, you're taught prayer principles and given opportunities to springboard into prayer. You can listen to the whole thing or just snatches of it. If you want to spend more time in prayer you can switch the tape off. By frequent use of the tapes you can absorb the teaching and move into dynamic prayer.

If you want to pray intelligently for world needs and become a global Christian, get hold of Patrick Johnstone's book, *Operation World*. You pray for a country a day, and you're informed of details about the nation for the day and given specific prayer targets to shoot at.

5

Dead End?

I was involved in 'Street Invaders', a BYFC summer evangelism project. This involved hordes of teenage Holy Ghost Rambos coming on board for a week of residential training, followed by three weeks of front-line evangelism. Morag, my wife, and our daughter, Naomi, were with me for the training slot. However, they were not going on mission with me.

The time came for Morag and Naomi to head back home. I borrowed a friend's car and drove them to Kidderminster railway station. From there we made the journey to Birmingham New Street Station where I saw them off on a Glasgow train. I returned to Kidderminster on the next train to drive back to Cleobury Place.

However, to get back to HQ this exiled Scotsman had to negotiate the rural roads which wind through the wilds of Worcestershire. I remember I hadn't taken a right turn, which I duly did. The route did seem a bit unfamiliar, and the road began to get narrower and narrower. I soon discovered I had gone down a farm track and could go no further. I was in a jam. I managed a tricky thirty-three point turn and headed back on course.

Every motorist at some point has doubtless had the same frustrating experience of taking a wrong turning. You carry on down the road oblivious to your navigational error. Next thing you know—you discover that you've driven down the road to nowhere. You can go no further! Cul de sac! Dead end. Whether it's a storm, a felled tree, a dirt track that vanishes, or a brick wall—no further progress is possible.

Maybe your praying is like that. You're in a rut. You feel as if your prayers don't even penetrate the ceiling, never mind touch the heart of God. Somehow you've been deflected from the path of effective prayer. Somewhere you took a wrong turn, and your praying is a dead-end experience.

We've all had the exasperating brick wall experience of finding we can go no further. Somehow we don't get through to God when we pray. We feel like that desperate figure in the Old Testament who complained: 'I cry out to you, O God, but you do not answer; I stand up, but you merely look at me' (Job 30:20).

OK then, let's look at some pitfalls for the prayer warrior. Let's explore some of the ways in which our praying can become a cul-de-sac experience. We're also going to see how we can negotiate the obstacles which thwart the path of effective prayer. You don't have to live in a dead-end street when it comes to prayer!

Blab and grab raid?

The local supermarket runs a competition. You vote for the shop assistant of the year. In twenty-five words or less you must explain your choice. The prize? All that you can stuff in your trolley in two minutes! The management lets you loose—pick what you like! Pile it high while the clock races on. The whistle will shriek full time. All the goodies you can grab in that allotted sliver of time are yours!

Our prayer life can come to a dead end if we treat God as the Celestial Supermarket Manager who ushers us to a turbo-charged prayer trolley. With an eye on the clock we hurtle through our blab-and-grab raid.

If we neglect praise, worship, adoration and thanksgiving, our prayer life will stagnate. If we don't see prayer as the pathway to intimacy with our heavenly Father, cultivating a relationship with Jesus, our Friend, we will get side-tracked into sounding off our self-centred shopping lists.

The late Keith Green lamented this me-centred trend: 'Bless me Lord, bless me Lord, you know that's all I ever hear. No one weeps, no one aches, no one even sheds one tear.'

Now, don't get me wrong. God wants to bless his children. Father wants to shower us with good things. 'He who did not spare his own Son, but gave him up for us all—how will he not also, along with him, graciously give us all things?' (Rom 8:32). But our priority must be getting closer to the Giver and not just gift-grabbing on our trolley raids.

Dad is away from home periodically on business trips. He never comes back empty-handed. There are always surprise souvenirs for his kids. How does he feel when consistently the first words that fall on his ears are: 'What did you get for me, Dad?' How does he feel when the children unwrap their presents, play with their toys and ignore him. It's 'Gimme. Gimme'—not 'Daddy, I love you. Dad, I missed you. Dad, it's great to see you.'

Father God delights in hearing our cries, 'Abba! Lord, I love you.' It's good to sprinkle our praying with singing—declaring our love and thanksgiving and gratitude to God. 'Sing and make music in your heart to the Lord, always giving thanks to God the Father for everything in the name of our Lord Jesus Christ' (Eph 5:19–20). Our praying should be focused on our God and not on ourselves.

We can also avoid stagnant, self-orientated, dead-end

prayer by getting stuck into the business of praying for others and other people's needs. Cultivating intimacy with God and a commitment to intercede for others will steer you away from a self-absorbed prayer life.

Life in the fast lane

You can get unstuck if you come rocketing into the prayer closet and rush back out. The Lord says to us, 'Be still, and know that I am God' (Ps 46:10). The hymn writer G. C. Stebbin's advice is:

Take time to be holy, speak oft with thy Lord.
Take time to be holy, the world rushes on.
Spend much time in secret with Jesus alone.
Take time to be holy, let him by thy Guide;
And run not before Him whatever betide.
Take time to be holy, be calm in thy soul.

Get the message? Bramwell Tripp put it this way: 'We cannot expect heartwarming fellowship if we rush in and rush out of God's presence.'

If you've been harpooned by Cupid's arrow, the ultimate dumb question to ask yourself is probably: how romantic can I be in sixty seconds? The thought of high speed sweet nothings whispered in your girlfriend's ear as you skateboard past her seems a trifle daft. Why then treat God that way?

Psychiatrist C. G. Jung once remarked, 'Hurry is not of the devil, it is the Devil.'[13] Our problem is we are a generation of white rabbit Christians, straight out of *Alice in Wonderland*. We scurry around with our clock in hand, announcing, 'I'm late, I'm late for a very important date. No time to say hello, goodbye! I'm late. I'm late. I'm late.'

A harassed spirit will not be conducive to effective prayer. Isaiah 30:15 might indicate something of a recipe for successful praying: '...in quietness and trust is your strength.'

Maybe we need to bring on board the words of 'the Preacher': 'Do not be quick with your mouth, do not be hasty in your heart to utter anything before God' (Eccles 5:2).

We live in the culture of the microwave. We get uptight if we have to wait more than five minutes for our food. We don't like waiting in a line in a post office or a super-market. If we want something, we expect to get it now. Sometimes we can run our lives at a frantic pace, crammed with activity. In the midst of all this, learn to take time to settle down in God's presence when you pray. If you're uptight when you pray, take time to calm down. Surrender your tensions, frustrations and hassles to the Lord.

We could do it

We will hit a dead end if *we* can put hands and feet to our prayers and we don't. Don't expect God to step in and do something that is our responsibility to get on with.

God's frozen people are huddled together for pep talk and prayer. It's barely fifteen minutes to kick-off at Ebenezer Tabernacle's 'Sunday Night Gospel Hour'. Reginald Rigormortis waxes eloquent: 'Our gracious mer-ciful God and Father in heaven, we beseech thee, bring in the unregenerate, draw sinners into this thy house tonight we implore thee, that they might come under the sound of the glorious gospel and receive thy precious word....'

The prayer is punctuated by 'Ah-mens' from Percy Pumblott. Thankfully, God can understand the prayer (being around before 1611 helps a great deal). Will he answer the prayer? Will the Almighty send in sinners to the 'Gospel Hour'? Why should God prod sinners in the direction of Ebenezer Tabernacle when the believers have not invited their friends? Why should an angel abseil down from heaven to drag kids in off the streets when they are ignored and passed by ET members headed for the evening service?

Many months ago I heard a raw, baby Christian share what God was doing in his life at a youth meeting. He explained how he tried to involve God in the tidying of the house. He prayed, 'Lord, I'll do the living room—give it a clean—and you do the dishes. OK?' Having set the living room in order he entered the kitchen and got a terrible shock. He was confronted by a pile of grotty dishes. God had not done the washing up. You're probably not too surprised by that. However, the aforementioned new Christian was bewildered.

Maybe you're a lot more sophisticated. You don't expect the Creator of the universe to wade into the kitchen debris. But it's exam time—you pray that God will bless you and give you success. If you have not studied and applied yourself, your 'prayer' is merely an expression of futile superstition. 'Faith without deeds is dead' (Jas 2:26).

Don't expect God to step in and do that which you and I are perfectly capable of doing ourselves. In the run-up to an evangelistic mission he was conducting, D. L. Moody attended the prayer meeting. Christians had gathered together to invite God to bless their outreach. Several rich folk were present, and one wealthy man prayed that God would release finances to meet the mission budget. D. L. Moody interrupted the rich man and brought his praying to an abrupt end. 'We don't need to trouble God about that, we are able to answer that prayer.'

Luke, in Luke 10 describes a prayer meeting that Jesus organised with seventy-two of his followers. He brought a specific request, 'Ask the Lord of the harvest, therefore, to send out workers into his harvest field' (Luke 10:2). The seventy-two set to prayer with great enthusiasm. Jesus stopped the prayer meeting.

'Men, I've got good news and bad news.'

'Oh really, Jesus? Tell us the good news first.'

'Father has heard your prayer.'

'He has? Hallelujah! That's fantastic. Thank you, Jesus. What's the bad news then, Lord?'

'Go! I am sending *you* as lambs among wolves.'

The seventy-two were the answers to their own prayers. True prayer is never a cop-out. Prayer means we are drawn into participation in the purposes of God.

Out of bounds

George has the hots for Helen. Every time she wiggles past him in the cafeteria his heart ricochets around his ribcage, his palms get damp and a lump the size of a basketball appears in his throat. It's difficult to concentrate in algebra classes. Why? A mere four desks away is that celestial vision of loveliness, Helen. George is a blood-bought, blood-washed, born again, redeemed child of the King of kings. Helen is not a Christian. Helen does not love Jesus. But, Helen likes George. George, being a man of prayer, enters his prayer closet where he asks for divine guidance. God has already given his verdict on the proposed relationship in the Bible. (Have a look at 2 Corinthians 6:14—7:1, Judges 13—16, 1 Kings 11:1–5, Ezra 9:1ff, Nehemiah 13:23ff). Father doesn't like it when his kids date unbelievers.

God has already revealed his will in the Scriptures. George's praying is a waste of time. God has spoken. If we get outside the boundaries of the Bible God will turn a deaf ear to our petitions. It does not matter how energetic our gymnastics are in the prayer closet. If we pray outside the will of God, quite simply he will not answer!

'This is the assurance we have in approaching God:

81

that if we ask anything *according to his will*, he hears us. And if we know that he hears us—whatever we ask—we know that we have what we asked of him' (1 Jn 5:14–15, italics mine). The Living Bible puts it this way: 'And we are sure of this, that he will listen to us whenever we ask him for anything in line with his will.'

We are to pray in submission to God's will—just like Jesus taught us. We are to pray: 'Your will be done' (Mt 6:10). This is the kind of praying Jesus engaged in at Gethsemane prior to his arrest—prayer in line with the will of the Father. John Stott has said, 'Every true prayer is a variation on the theme: "Your will be done".'

When we do pray in line with God's will, we can pray with boldness and confidence that he hears us.

Keep at it

We will not see instant results every time we pray. Pot Noodles are an instant snack or meal. Just add boiling water, stir well and they're ready to eat. Prayer is not a spiritual Pot Noodle. It's not simply a case of adding lots of boiling faith and stirring ourselves to pray with enthusiasm.

It's helpful to remind ourselves that Jesus has commanded us to pray and not give up (Lk 18:1). He calls us to pray with persistence. God calls us to stick at it in prayer.

> I have posted watchmen on your walls O Jerusalem;
> they *will never be silent* day or night.
> You who call on the Lord, *give yourselves no rest,*
> *and give him no rest* till he establishes Jerusalem
> and makes her the praise of the earth (Is 62:6–7, italics mine).

Prayer is not charismatic fun and games. Praying can be a difficult, tiresome business. In Exodus 17 Moses found that praying for the victory of God's people in battle requires an investment of time and energy. Moses did not simply pray a prayer and accept that the answer would happen. He prayed until victory was secure and found the whole business exhausting. But Moses kept at it!

George Muller was a great prayer warrior who saw remarkable answers to prayer. Muller knew that we must pray and not give up. Muller persisted in prayer until the answer came. Muller knew the secret of keeping at it. Muller prayed for over sixty years that a man would be converted. More than sixty years on he is praying for his friend. Muller commented, 'He is not saved but will be. How can it be otherwise, I am praying?' After Muller died the friend was converted!

Check the vertical and horizontal hold

There's a world of a difference between saying prayers and praying. Praying comes out of our relationship with God. If there is a breakdown in our relationship with the Lord, our praying will be futile—merely an exercise in generating hot air.

'We know that God does not listen to sinners. He listens to the godly man who does his will' (Jn 9:31). If we do not have a personal relationship with Jesus, if our sin has not been dealt with and our sins forgiven—prayer will be a disaster.

Perhaps you are a genuine child of God. You have had an authentic Jesus experience. But you find that you are parked in a dead end with your prayer life going nowhere. The issue could be unconfessed sin. King David was aware that undealt with sin meant unanswered prayer. 'He [God] would not have listened if I had not confessed my sins' (Ps 66:18, TLB).

Sin is a barrier between us and God. Sin is a blockade to answered prayer. The bad news is, if you are not right with God your praying is on the road to nowhere. The good news is, the blood of Jesus cleanses us from all sin (1 Jn 1:7).

Walking clean with God is a prerequisite to effective prayer. Psalm 32:6 instructs, '...let everyone who is godly pray...' James tells us, 'The earnest prayer of a righteous man has great power and wonderful results' (Jas 5:16, TLB).

You might find it helpful to stop reading for a moment. Take time to invite the Holy Spirit to put the floodlights on any areas in your life which displease God.

> Who may ascend the hill of the Lord?
> Who may stand in his holy place?
> He who has clean hands and a pure heart,
> who does not lift up his soul to an idol
> or swear by what is false.
> He will receive blessing from the Lord... (Ps 24:3–5a).

Now, don't get all introspective. Don't poke around your spiritual innards looking for something that needs sorting. Allow God to do it. Allow the Lord to turn his X-ray machine on. If he shows you areas that need to be dealt with, confess your sin. Invite Jesus to cleanse you. Put things right. You may have to seek someone's forgiveness and make good any damage you may have done. Get to it. When you stand before God with clean hands and a pure heart you will have power in your praying.

God is not a cosmic great uncle who roars at our naughty little wrongdoings. God is absolutely holy. God hates sin. Sin is a barrier to fellowship with God. Someone said, 'Anyone who would have power in prayer must be merciless in dealing with his own sins.'

Have you ever had the frustrating experience of your TV going *kaput* at the climactic moment of the latest instalment of your favourite programme? Instant snow. Diagonal lines dance across the screen. But, all is not lost.

You fiddle with the vertical hold, and then—*bingo!* An adjustment of horizontal hold and your programme is back on the box.

For effective prayer to take place we must ensure that both vertical and horizontal hold are in proper alignment in our lives. What do I mean? Jesus told us our Christian lives are two dimensional. Jesus said, 'Love the Lord your God with all your heart, soul, mind and strength'—that's the vertical relationship. Jesus had more to say: 'And'— here comes the horizontal—'love your neighbour as yourself.'

The Bible stresses the need for us to have right relationships if we want to be pray-ers who make contact with God. Resentment, bitterness, withholding forgiveness, bearing grudges—all are ingredients in the recipe for a barren prayer life.

The apostle Peter points this out in the context of marriage:

> Husbands in the same way be considerate as you live with your wives, and treat them with respect as the weaker partner and as heirs with you of the gracious gift of life, so that nothing will hinder your prayers' (1 Pet 3:7).

Your response is, 'That's fine, but I'm not married and I don't plan to get married.' The point is, here is a principle which applies to all of us regardless of our marital status. The quality of our relationships determines the effectiveness of our praying.

If a church or fellowship or your youth group is splintered by quarreling or unforgiving people, then the Enemy gains an entrance (take a look at 2 Corinthians 2:10–11). Jesus hits us with some solemn words which we can't just 'spiritualise' away: 'Your heavenly Father will forgive you if you forgive those who sin against you; but if *you* refuse to forgive *them*, *he* will not forgive *you*' (Mt 6:14–15, TLB).

Mark puts it this way: 'But when you are praying, first

forgive anyone you are holding a grudge against, so that your Father in heaven will forgive you your sins too' (Mk 11:25, TLB).

God will not extend mercy to those who withhold forgiveness. Jesus taught us to pray in his pattern prayer: '...forgive our sins—for we have forgiven those who sinned against us' (Lk 11:4, TLB).

When Peter came to Jesus and asked, 'Lord, how many times shall I forgive my brother when he sins against me? Up to seven times?', Jesus' response was, 'Peter, you and I must be forgiveness unlimited people.'

Paul instructed the Ephesian Christians, 'Be kind and compassionate to one another, forgiving each other, just as in Christ God forgave you' (Eph 4:32).

If someone hurts you, do not cling onto what they have done to you. Let go of it. Let go of 'your right' to be offended and forgive them. God does not keep a score card—he does not want you to either. Come to him in prayer and tell the Lord you forgive the person who brought you injury, and release them to the Lord. An unforgiving spirit is the way to self-destruction. An unforgiving spirit means that when we approach God in prayer he turns a deaf ear to us.

You need to give up the right to strike back at the person who hurt you. You need to surrender 'the right' and any plans to damage the person who damaged you. This will not always be easy. More often it will be quite difficult. Don Francisco used to sing: 'Love is not an emotion, it's an act of your will.' This is true forgiveness. Forgiving someone is not a feeling, it's a commitment. It is a decision you make, and until you decide to release the person whom you're withholding forgiveness from—until you decide to forgive—your praying will permanently be parked in a dead-end street.

If you are a Jesus person, a real Christian, then you are part of a kingdom of royal priests with right of access into

God's very presence. Back in Old Testament times, right of access to God's presence was for restricted personnel only. A large, thick curtain blocked people out of the Holy of Holies. Only the high priest could make an annual entrance. The good news is that when Jesus died for our sins '...the curtain of the temple was torn in two from the top to the bottom' (Mt 27:51). A top-down torn curtain! God made the first move. God took the initiative and every child of God has the priestly right to enter God's presence. Jesus' shed blood is our guarantee of right of access (Heb 10:19).

We need to remember that Old Testament priests performed their ministry as men who purified themselves and were ceremonially clean. Think about it. Are you clean before God? If you're a Christian you have access to God. Are you coming clean?

To believe or not to believe—that is the question

Our praying must be fuelled by confidence in the living God. Unbelief will be a sure way of guaranteeing our prayers do not penetrate the ceiling. Hebrews 11:6 tells us, 'And without faith it is impossible to please God, because anyone who comes to him must believe that he exists and that he rewards those who earnestly seek him.'

Perhaps you come to God in a half-hearted way, unsure of whether or not he is listening to your prayer and uncertain that he will answer. Don't be surprised if you find yourself in a prayer cul-de-sac.

Effective prayer is built on confidence in God. Jesus exhibited confidence in the Father in his ministry. Prior to commanding life into Lazarus's corpse and summoning him out of the tomb, Jesus prayed. It was a faith-filled prayer. Jesus offered thanks to his Father for Lazarus being raised from the dead—before it happened! Jesus said, 'Father, I thank you that you have heard me. I knew that you always hear me...' (Jn 11:41–42). That is confidence in the Father!

When we pray we should do so with an attitude of expectancy. God is 'able to do immeasurably more than all we ask or imagine' (Eph 3:20).

Our praying should be characterised by godly confidence and holy audacity. 'Let us then approach the throne of grace with confidence, so that we may receive mercy and find grace to help us in our time of need' (Heb 4:16).

If you want fuel for your faith, read the word of God. '...faith cometh by hearing, and hearing by the word of God' (Rom 10:17, KJV). The word of God reveals the will of God—this is the foundation of our confidence. Our prayer confidence is rooted in the character of God—he keeps his word. The antidote to feeble faith or uncertain praying is to consult the word of God on the issue concerned. When we find out what God says we can proceed accordingly.

Praying in line with the will of God should fill us with holy aggression. We have been instructed to pray. 'Come kingdom of God; be done will of God!' Praying for God's will to be executed is inviting God to do what he wants to do. God is waiting for those on earth to come into agreement with his will and to invite him to step in. God is not reluctant to do his will, so when you pray in line with the will of God, be confident God will answer!

Unbelief is the enemy of effective prayer. In James 5 we find instruction on the church's healing ministry. He tells us, '...the prayer offered in faith will make the sick person well; the Lord will raise him up' (Jas 5:15).

Faith makes the difference. Jesus told blind Bartimaeus, 'Your faith has healed you' (Mk 10:52). When Jesus was approached by two men for healing, 'he touched their eyes and said, "According to your faith will it be done to you" ' (Mt 9:29).

I need to stress that we shouldn't have faith in our faith.

Faith involves trusting in God, taking him at his word and resting in his integrity. While unbelieving prayer is futile, it is not 'our faith' that gets results. It is God who answers the prayers of his childrlen.

'All those who know your mercy, Lord, will count on you for help. For you have never yet forsaken those who trust in you' (Ps 9:10, TLB). We can count on God. He will never abandon us. If you find yourself praying for someone or an issue in your life, measure your prayer aim against the word of God. Consult the Bible on the matter. If your prayer desire is in line with the word of God, stand on the word, declare the word in your praying...go for it!

Why am I praying?

One of the reasons our prayers go unanswered is selfishness. Wrong motives can destroy effective prayer. 'You do not have, because you do not ask God. When you ask, you do not receive, because you ask with wrong motives, that you may spend what you get on your pleasures' (Jas 4:2–3).

Here we discover that you don't get answers if you don't pray. Also, *why* we come to God in prayer is vital. R. A. Torrey said, 'The chief purpose of prayer is that God may be glorified in the answer.'

During a mission I was leading, I went into a park where a lot of young people hang out. I met a young man who had drifted from the church. We'll call him George. I led George to Jesus. Later on I met up with his 'Christian' flatmate who was thrilled that George had got right with God. The reason he was happy was not particularly because George was lost and had been found. This guy was chuffed because life in the flat would now be smoother. Selfishness!

Selfishness like that can very easily seep into our prayers. It's very subtle because it can pollute a very

legitimate aim. Your spouse or parents may not appreci-
ate the fact that you love Jesus. As a result they make life
at home for the sole Christian there (you) very difficult. If
your prayers for their salvation are fuelled by a desire for
them to give you peace and quiet 'you ask with wrong
motives'.

A youth leader prays that the church's youth ministry
flourishes. He prays that the droves of heathen who
occupy the youth club are converted. His praying is quite
legitimate—these kids desperately need Jesus. But Mr
Youth Worker's praying is not energised by the love of
God. His praying is motivated by a desire to be seen as a
successful youth worker. Will God honour such prayer?

Leonard Ravenhill has remarked that if John Knox had
prayed, 'God give me success' we would never have heard
of him. But John Knox prayed, 'Give me Scotland or I
die!'

Jesus' promise is, 'I will do whatever you ask in my
name, so that the Son may bring glory to the Father' (Jn
14:13). Jesus' chief concern in answering our prayers is to
honour his Father. The goal of your life, your ambition
and the purpose of your praying should be to glorify God.

John Allan throws down a challenge on our prayer
motivation:

> Praying earnestly for the conversion of the blonde bombshell
> next door, rather than spotty Fred up the street, is an easy
> trap for Christian males to fall into! How unselfish are your
> prayers? God can't honour prayers with ulterior motives. If
> your motives are confused and mixed, admit it honestly to
> him and carry on praying anyway.[14]

Action stations

I've outlined some areas that can frustrate our praying.
The list is not exhaustive. Later on in the context of
developing a personal prayer habit and in looking at

prayer warfare we will pick up on some other issues which can nullify effective prayer.

But right now take stock. Invite God to show you if there are things to clear up. Take a personal inventory. Identify those areas we have looked at which are barriers in your own life to effective prayer. Now take action! Take the steps necessary to dismantle the barriers and move on to the place where God can honour your praying.

6

Being a Bridge

As we have discovered already, prayer has different elements and ingredients. Prayer is a means of cultivating intimacy with our heavenly Father. We have the privilege of bringing our own cares, concerns and needs to God in prayer. Our loving Father is interested in every detail of our lives. It is quite legitimate to bring your own needs to God in prayer. Jesus instructed us to do so. Jesus told us to pray, 'Give us this day our daily bread.'

When Morag and I were students together at theological cemetery...er...seminary, we did not have a lot of money. Our only income was one student grant: Morag's. I was not eligible for a grant because I had previously completed another degree course. If you are a student you will know that the government is not overflowing with generosity to students. Grants don't go far at all. Morag had been to the opticians and needed glasses. She was walking down the road praying, 'Lord, where will we get the money for my glasses?' As she walked towards the flat, she was bringing her need to God. I came to meet Morag on the street. In my hand was a cheque we had just received in the post which covered the cost of the spectacles. 'Your Father knows what you need before you ask him' (Mt 6:8).

We are commanded to bring all the things that trouble

us to God in prayer. Hassles and heartaches? The Bible declares, 'Cast all your anxiety on him because he cares for you' (1 Pet 5:7). Keith Green sang, 'No sin is too big; no problem too small—Jesus is Lord of all.'

However, we have a responsibility before God to pray for other people and their needs. God invites us not only to have fellowship with him and bring our needs to him—he wants us to be involved in implementing his will on earth. God wants us to be pray-ers who inflict eternal damage on the kingdom of darkness. God wants you and me to enforce his will in the here and now through prayer.

True prayer is not an exercise in bringing to God just me, mine, myself and I. God has delegated his authority to us. We are the agents of his kingdom revolution. '...The kingdom of heaven has been forcefully advancing, and forceful men lay hold of it' (Mt 11:12). God calls us to holy violence—to forceful prayer. Father doesn't want a bunch of self-absorbed pray-ers—he looks for us to get caught up in the purposes of his kingdom and to engage in kingdom praying. God wants you to stand up and fight against everything that is contrary to his perfect will. Prayer is the fight. You can punch holes in the darkness by getting hold of God in prayer.

God calls us to prayer advocacy. 'Speak up for those who cannot speak for themselves, for the rights of all who are destitute. Speak up and judge fairly; defend the rights of the poor and needy' (Prov 31:8–9). These sayings of King Lemuel are a clear indication that God wants his people to be committed to justice. God wants you to speak on behalf of the voiceless. This is what intercessory prayer involves. It involves bringing people's needs to God. Intercession involves pleading someone else's cause.

1 Samuel 2:25 poses a question: 'If a man sins against another man, God may mediate for him; but if a man sins against the Lord, who can intercede for him?' The parallelism in this verse shows us another aspect of intercession:

mediation. A mediator is a go-between who represents both parties' interests. When you intercede for someone you stand between them and God, representing them before God. As an intercessor you engage in the priestly ministry of bringing someone to God in prayer.

Maybe you've seen *Superman—The Movie*. As I write this there's been talk of Christopher Reeve pulling his tights back on for *Superman 5*. But I'm talking about the first in the series. Marlon Brando appears as Supe's dad. Brando discovers that the planet Krypton, where he lives, is in jeopardy. So little 'Superbaby' is placed into a rocket and propelled towards our planet just before Krypton explodes.

In no time at all Superbaby becomes Superboy, who grows into Superman. During the film, Superman's arch-enemy Lex Luthor activates the San Andreas Fault. There is incredible devastation. In one scene an express train hurtles down a track. The driver is ignorant of a huge gap torn in the bridge; carnage is inevitable. The train is just about to plunge into a chasm, when Superman comes to the rescue. He places himself in the gap and the train is able to pass over safely. Superman became a bridge.

God calls each of us to be a bridge. He calls us to position ourselves, in prayer, between God and man. God wants us to 'stand in the gap'.

God is searching for intercessors—those who by their selfless praying stand between two worlds. The Lord informs his prophet:

> I looked for a man among them who would build up the wall and stand before me in the gap on behalf of the land so that I would not have to destroy it, but I found none. So I will pour out my wrath on them and consume them with my fiery anger...' (Ezek 22:30–31).

The implications of what God said are devastating. The people had turned their backs on God as a nation. God wanted to avoid pouring out his wrath. God was looking for a means to avoid bringing about just judgement. So God went on a search for intercessors. God's recruitment drive drew a blank. The consequences? Judgement fell on the land. And judgement fell because there were no intercessors to avert it. If God had his 'bridges'—those to stand in the gap—judgement could have been avoided.

This episode in the life of Israel highlights how strategic intercession is. John Wesley said, 'God does nothing in this world except by prayer.' History can be altered by you approaching God in prayer. And clearly the here and now is affected if you do not approach God in prayer. Samuel was an intercessor who declared, 'God forbid that I should sin against the Lord in ceasing to pray for you...' (1 Sam 12:23, KJV). You can choose to be a changemaker by committing yourself to intercessory prayer.

Abraham prayed the first recorded intercessory prayer in the Bible. You can find it in Genesis 18:23–33. We discover that God confided in Abraham and revealed to him that he planned to destroy Sodom and Gomorrah (18:17–21). God confided in the intercessor! Abraham's response was to plead for the city. Abraham asked God to spare the city if there were fifty righteous people living in it. God agreed. Then Abraham asked if the city would be spared for the sake of forty-five, then forty, then thirty, then twenty. Abraham's final request was for judgement to be averted for the sake of just ten righteous people. God agreed to every request that his servant Abraham made.

Abraham's intercession was a mixture of holy boldness, humility and reverence. He boldly asked God, 'Will you sweep away the righteous with the wicked?' (18:23). Abraham was bold, but showed great honour and respect for his God. He said, '...I have been so bold to speak to the Lord, though I am nothing but dust and ashes...' (18:27). Abraham was confident, but he was not cocky in prayer. We can learn a great deal from Abraham the intercessor.

He was a man who would not give up. To be effective intercessors, we need to follow his persistent example. The Lord Jesus indicated that sometimes when we pray we only have to ask; other times we may have to seek to get an answer. And sometimes we may need to be even more persistent. 'Ask and it will be given to you; seek and you will find; knock and the door will be opened to you' (Mt 7:7; Lk 11:9).

Dave Bryant identifies three paces of intercession in his superb book, *With Concerts of Prayer*. Bryant says there is: (1) solidarity—agreeing with God; (2) advocacy—standing up for others; and (3) pursuit—pressing on for a change.[15]

Abraham not only stood up for the inhabitants of sin-soaked Sodom—he pressed God to change his plans. Abraham persistently pursued God.

We can learn not only from Abraham's persistence, but also from the grounds for his persistence. What made Abraham keep on 'nagging' God? What gave him the confidence? God's character was the grounds for Abraham's request. Abraham appealed to the integrity of God. 'Will not the Judge of all the earth do right?' (Gen 18:25). What we know about God gives us tremendous confidence when we pray to him. Abraham knew he was laying hold of God, who does not delight in pouring out judgement—a just, righteous and loving God who will always do right.

Lethal weapon

There is tremendous power in intercessory prayer. Jesus told his followers, 'All authority in heaven and on earth has been given to me' (Mt 28:18). This was the declaration of Jesus, the champion over evil. All authority belongs to Jesus. He has smashed the final enemy: death. He lives for ever by the power of his indestructible life. He is King. But there's more—in Luke 10, Jesus told the seventy-two, 'I have given you authority to trample on snakes and scorpions and to overcome all the power of the enemy; nothing will harm you' (Lk 10:19).

We share in the kingly authority of Jesus! Lethal weapon has got nothing to do with Danny Glover or Mel Gibson. We are lethal weapons in the hand of God when we pray! We wield royal heavenly authority when we pray. The lethal nature of prayer is demonstrated in an episode in the life of Moses (see Exodus 17:8–16).

The Israelites were minding their own business at Rephidim when they heard the roar of turbo-charged camels. The Amalekites had arrived. 'Come and have a go with the Amalekite aggro!' The Amalekites then waded into the Israelites. Moses decided to take action. He got hold of Joshua. 'Josh, go get hold of some of the men and go and fight the Amalekites.'

'Sure thing, boss. Where will you be, sir?'

'I will be standing on top of the hill, Joshua,' replied Moses.

Now, you might be thinking, 'That's pretty clever!' Moses sends Joshua and some of Israel's finest into the thick of battle on the plain. Moses perches on a hilltop watching the spectacle from a distance. Wrong!

Moses *was* in the thick of the action. Moses held the strategic role in the whole military operation. It's what Moses did on the hilltop that was the key. On the day the Amalekites mounted their surprise attack on Israel, Moses announced, 'Tomorrow I will stand on top of the hill with the staff of God in my hands' (Ex 17:9).

The staff of God was symbolic of the authority that God had invested in his servant, Moses. We find that, 'As long as Moses held up his hands, the Israelites were winning, but whenever he lowered his hands, the Amalekites were winning' (Ex 17:11). What was going on?

The outcome of the military conflict was being settled by Moses' prayer. There was fierce fighting on the field of combat, but it was not swordplay that would secure victory for Israel. The intercession of a man in tune with God was what won the day. Moses was participating in the first recorded prayer triplet. He had company on the hilltop. He had Aaron and Hur to support him. These two men saw Moses tiring. Intercession is hard work! Aaron and Hur got a boulder for Moses to sit on. They held his hands steady until sunset. As a result of the hilltop activity, '...Joshua overcame the Amalekite army with the sword' (Ex 17:13).

To celebrate military success, Moses built an altar to God. He called it: 'The Lord is my Banner of Victory' (Jehovah Nissi). Moses clearly recognised that the battle belonged to the Lord. The Lord God had defeated the Amalekites. But Moses had to pray. Moses had aligned himself with God's purposes and enforced the will of God on the battlefield by praying for Israel. He exercised his God-given authority by lifting his hands to God in prayer.

In our intercession we do the same. We align ourselves with God's perfect will, exercise our royal authority in prayer and enforce the will of God. We pray, 'Come, kingdom of God! Be done, will of God!' Intercessory prayer is your lethal weapon. Prayer is the means by which God is justified in intervening in any circumstance or situation. When we pray, we are saying to the God of heaven, 'Invade, Lord! Lord, we give you the right to break in here.'

You can take hold of something and pray the will of God into it. Lynne and Kay were two Christian girls concerned about the goings-on in their school. Their school had an officially sanctioned Dungeons and Dragons club. D and D is a fantasy role playing game that can open up the participants to destructive demonic influences. These two fine godly girls knew that.

They were upset and came to me for advice. I phoned the Evangelical Alliance who told me that the wisest course of action would be for concerned parents to make an approach. No concerned parents, Christian or otherwise, got involved. However, Lynne and Kay got involved. They prayed. They interceded for their schoolfriends and prayed against the club. The school shut down the Dungeons and Dragons society.

My friend and colleague John Markin and I were doing a schools mission in a town. John is a very fine musician. You might have come across him at events like Spring Harvest or bought his albums. He communicates the love of Jesus in a very effective way through his excellent music. Our plan was very simple. We got access to assemblies and lunch-time clubs with the aim of drawing the school kids to an evangelistic event in a local college. John would play and I would preach at the college event. We took classes, assemblies and did some lunch-time events. We worked the area for about ten days.

One school was proving impossible to get access into. The Christian teachers on the school were not willing to approach the head teacher. However, one young man in the school took action. He prayed, 'Lord, this is garbage. I believe it's your will that Bill and Johnny get into this school to communicate something of the gospel. Make it possible. Open a door of opportunity.'

He then put feet to his praying. Intercession leads to action. Peter approached the head teacher and explained what Johnny and I were doing in the area. He asked the head teacher if we could do a presentation in the school.

The head teacher cancelled the period after lunch to enable us to have about forty-five minutes or an hour. The kids could come if they wanted to. If they didn't want to—well, they had an extra-long lunch.

The school hall was packed with kids who were very evidently enjoying Johnny's presentation. I sat there praying and thinking, 'How do I follow this? How will they cope with the talking head?' I got up to deliver my talk, and the presence of God descended on the place. The kids listened to what I had to say with attentiveness. When I opened up question time, the questions provided clear opportunities for the good news to be shared. The school was buzzing. Obviously visitors, one of whom is an exceptional musician, would cause a stir. But it was more than that. I went upstairs to see a teacher. As I entered the room a boy was asking, 'Sir, Jesus was a Christian, wasn't he?'

All of that happened because Peter took action. He prayed to God.

Andy Kennedy, a worker with YWAM, was involved as a youngster in heading up the Scripture Union at his school with another pupil. They decided to make things happen by praying. They organised meetings in the mornings where they would pray for the conversion of their non-Christian class-mates. Loads of young folk began to follow Jesus as a result. Andy and the other leader were hauled before the Head who wanted to know if they were organising a takeover of the school! Intercession works.

I was in Poland with John Markin and his wife Darlene. I was doing some Bible teaching and evangelistic preaching. The focus of our trip was a youth camp. During my first evangelistic preach I was aware of the Lord's presence in a very powerful way. I invited those who wanted to give their lives to Jesus to stay behind in the tent. There was a 'holy hush' in the place, which was not broken by people leaving the tent. It was as if the stillness of God had fallen in the tent. Some folk stayed behind. The others silently slipped out into the night. I've seen greater responses to the preaching of the gospel, but I experienced a very unique sense of the presence of God. I was preaching on a Tuesday night. My home church's prayer meeting is on a Tuesday night. Due to the one hour time difference my church was praying for me while I was preaching. I'm convinced that their intercession made the difference. Their praying released the presence of God hundreds of miles away!

God calls you to engage in intercession. He wants you to be a bridge between heaven and earth, between eternity and the here and now. Reinhard Bonnke says, 'Intercessors are mighty battering rams.'[16] Energised by the Spirit of the living God, you can be a battering ram! You can be involved in assaulting the gates of hell by being an intercessory battering ram. You can gouge holes in the kingdom of darkness and be an agent of God's kingdom.

Down through history God has raised up young battering rams to assault the kingdom of darkness in prayer.

Little Lutz was one of God's battering rams. Count Ludwig von Zinzendorf, to give him his proper name and title. He became a Christian when he was a little lad. From an early age he enjoyed talking to Jesus. He told his friends about Jesus and organised prayer meetings. He became a 'global Christian' early on—he had a passionate desire to make Jesus known throughout the world. When he was ten years old he got together with five of his pals and formed a missionary society. They called it the Order of the Grain of Mustard Seed. His objectives were to encourage Christians to help the persecuted and take the gospel to those who had never heard it.

When he was older he founded Herrnhut, 'The Lord's Watch'. It struggled to get off the ground. He tried to get Christians together from various backgrounds, and initially Herrnhut was jeopardised by quarreling and division. It only survived termination because of a tremendous visitation of the Holy Spirit. As the Holy Spirit released the love of God (Rom 5:5), the believers were fused together. A prayer meeting was sparked off that lasted for 100 years—an unbroken chain! Herrnhut really became the Lord's watch! The Moravians became a tremendous missionary force, doubtless because those in Herrnhut were pleading to the Lord of the harvest to send workers out into the fields. The Moravians, of which Zinzendorf was a leader, were so committed to world evangelisation that some of them became slaves so that the gospel could go where white men were forbidden. Their motto was, 'That the Lamb who was slain might receive the reward of the fruit of his suffering.' Zinzendorf is reported to have said, 'I have one passion—it is he [Jesus].' Such devotion to Jesus and commitment to the advancement of the gospel was fuelled in the fires of intercession.

David Brainerd was a young man who enjoyed the dubious privilege of being ejected from Bible college. He was asked what he thought of the college principal. He offered his opinion: 'He's got as much grace as the leg of that chair.' Word spread, and despite the shedding of many tears, he was out the door. He did not have a great start to ministry! He was a cold, indifferent Christian who got heated up by the Holy Spirit. He began to gain a passion to reach the American Indians. But he had a problem! He could not speak the lingo. He had another problem. His interpreter was very fond of firewater! How would you like to preach the gospel with the help of a sozzled interpreter? What did Brainerd do? He prayed. He got hold of God. He pleaded for an outpouring of the Spirit. He interceded for the lost Indians, cut off from the living God.

Brainerd would go out into the fields and pray. In the winter he would kneel in the snow. This, doubtless, was a big factor in his untimely death. Brainerd died of TB when he was only twenty-nine. Before he got promoted to heaven, he witnessed a Holy Spirit hurricane pulling the Indians into God's kingdom.

Charles Finney saw extraordinary fruit in his ministry. 80% of his converts went on with God and never backslid. He saw revival fire ignited through his anointed preaching. He saw communities shaken by spiritual awakening.

One of the secrets of this dynamic ministry had to be a bloke called Nash. Nash would often accompany Finney. If you'd been in town you probably would never have guessed Nash existed. However, heaven and hell knew Nash was around. He devoted himself to praying down God's blessing.

God is committed to his intercessors. Take time to read Norman Grubb's book, *Rees Howells: Intercessor*. It is the remarkable story of how intercession changes history— even the course of events in World War II! The National Director of British Youth for Christ, Lowell Sheppard, and I sat in a minister's home in the Hebrides. The minister's mother-in-law was there. He informed us that she was one of the church's battleships—in the nicest possible way, of course. No, this man of God was not about to unleash his repertoire of mother-in-law jokes. He matter-of-factly told us, 'She's one of our battleships— she's a prayer warrior.' This dear old saint reached across and grasped Lowell's hand and whispered, 'Prayer wins wars. I know, I've proved it.'

Prayer wins wars—will you join the war effort? God wants prayer warriors to stand in the gap.

Evangelist Philip Jinadu is one such bridge. He made a tremendous impact for God in his school. The Jesus revolution that Philip was involved in flowed out of prayer. Philip met with some friends (they did not all attend the same school) for prayer. Their prayer agenda was simple: that God would break into their school and that their friends would be saved.

Philip started a Christian Union. Five folk turned up. Four got saved! Philip took an assembly in the school. He wanted the whole school to hear about Jesus before he left. Taking assembly was therefore an obvious part of his battle plan. He got up and sang at the piano an old Andrae Crouch number: 'Jesus is the Answer'. His classmates and others began to snear and snigger. Philip began to cry! He was not weeping out of embarrassment. As he sat at the piano, he experienced the power and presence of God in a unique way. He got up and offered a brief challenge. If folk had the guts to find out more about Jesus, be at the CU. The CU was packed—the revolution was under way! A revolution birthed in prayer. Philip later devised a prayer scheme. He drew up a hit list and prayed for each person until they were converted. Why not take a leaf out of his book?

Some years ago a group of young people, freshly baptised in the Holy Spirit, began to meet for prayer. They began to pray for their town. A vision for a town-wide outreach was born. The town hall was booked, and subsequently there was an evangelist. Church liaison involved getting the venue and then getting local leaders. That's called the cart before the horse. The town hall was packed, sinners were converted, and the gospel was taken onto the streets and into shipyards and factories. I could tell you lots of exciting stories—but I won't! God moved because some young folk, filled with the Spirit, got into the bridge business. God talks to us. They were stupid enough not only to listen, but to do what God said. Intercession leads to action. Schools and towns can be impacted when you pray, listen and obey.

God calls you to make a difference by your intercession. On January 21, 1930, King George addressed the opening session of the London Naval Arms Conference. It was a historic occasion. It was to be broadcast on radio. It was to be a global broadcast. Across the world people could pick up the voice of King George. The United States almost missed the whole thing. Just before the king took to the airwaves, someone at CBS tripped over and snapped a wire. The result was that the connections to the king were cut.

Harold Vivian was in the control room. He reached out and grabbed the ends of the wires. When he did that, the circuit was complete. Electricity surged through his body. And the king's speech was broadcast after all.[17]

The circuit between God and man has been broken. God wants you to stand in the gap through intercessory prayer. God wants you to make contact with him and at the same time to identify with the needs of your world.

To be effective in intercession you need a heart that is filled with the love of God. You need a heart filled with compassion—a heart that beats with the heart-beat of the living God. When Lowell Sheppard, BYFC's National Director, was a teenager he met Bob Pierce, the founder of World Vision. Lowell asked Bob, 'Mr Pierce, how can I become a man of God?'

Bob Pierce responded, 'Find out what is breaking the heart of God and pray that it will break your heart also.'

The intercessor has pain in her heart because she feels the pain in the heart of God.

Just before the global flood, Scripture records:

> The Lord saw how great man's wickedness on the earth had become, and that every inclination of the thoughts of his heart was only evil all the time. The Lord was grieved that he had made man on the earth, and his heart was filled with pain (Gen 6:5–6).

The intercessor hurts when God is hurting. This is because intercession is not mechanically praying for other people's needs. In intercession we may share in Jesus' suffering. God puts his agenda in our hearts. We bring other people's needs before God. Effective intercession flows not only out of an intimate relationship with God, but identification with the person you're praying for and with their plight.

Moses was great in intercession because he not only had a passion for the will of God, but also radically identified with those he represented before God. He was a man with a burden.

Israel had built and offered worship to a golden calf. This was an open act of rebellion against God. It was the Lord who delivered them out of slavery in Egypt, but they approached the golden calf with offerings and declared, 'This is your god, O Israel, who brought you up out of Egypt' (Ex 32:4, margin).

This did not escape God's notice. The Lord confides in his intercessors and he spoke to Moses. 'I have seen these people...and they are a stiff-necked people. Now leave me alone so that my anger may burn against them and that I may destroy them. Then I will make you into a great nation' (Ex 32:9–10).

How did Moses respond? 'I couldn't agree with you more. Wipe out the lot of them. Wow, I've always fancied becoming a great nation'? No—Moses showed no signs of self-interest or ambition. Out of concern for his people, '...Moses sought the favour of the Lord his God' (Ex 32:11). Moses pleaded in prayer on behalf of the rebellious Israelites. Moses mediated between Israel and God. He sought God for mercy on behalf of those who had betrayed the One who freed them from slavery.

Moses took Israel's side. He appealed to the character of God. This was serious business. God was not making an idle threat. Moses realised that. Moses told the Lord that if he destroyed the Israelites his reputation in Egypt would be jeopardised (Ex 32:12). Moses also called God to be faithful to what he promised Abraham, Isaac and Israel (Ex 32:13). Moses knew God keeps his promises so he called God to keep his word. The result of Moses's intercession was, '...the Lord relented and did not bring on his people the disaster he had threatened' (Ex 32:14).

But it's not enough to feel for people in their plight. An intercessor must see things from God's perspective. Moses felt deeply for his people. Moses was a man passionately in love with his God. If we love God, we will not only hurt when he hurts—we will hate what he hates. We will be angry if he is insulted. The Bible says, 'Be ye angry, and sin not' (Eph 4:26, KJV). When Moses returned from his meeting with God, the holy anger of the intercessor burned within him. God was being insulted by Israel's behaviour. Moses was upset!

When Moses approached the camp and saw the calf and the dancing, his anger burned and he threw the tablets out of his hands, breaking them to pieces at the foot of the mountain. And he took the calf they had made and burned it in the fire; then he ground it to powder, scattered it on the water and made the Israelites drink it (Ex 32:19–20).

As intercessor, Moses was a mediator. He was not just a spokesman for Israel. He was God's man. A mediator intervened between two parties. Job said, 'There is no umpire between us, to lay his hand upon us both' (Job 9:33, RSV). Moses was the umpire/arbitrator who stood between two worlds. He stood in the gap, simultaneously acting on God's behalf and Israel's behalf. He had laid his hand upon both—God and Israel. This is why Moses could not wimp out when it came to confronting Israel with her disobedience.

Aaron was quite prepared to soft pedal on the issue. 'Don't get too upset, bro. It's just the way they are, Moses. You know what they're like' (Ex 32:22, paraphrased!).

There could be no compromise with Moses. It's not enough to be 'compassionate'. The intercessor prays from God's vantage point. Feeling for Israel did not blur God's perspective. Moses had taken Israel's side against the Lord. Now he stood against the rebel nation on behalf of his God. He got hold of the Levites who on Moses' instruction waded through the camp wielding swords.

The Levites each killed his brother, his son, his friend. Much blood flowed. 3,000 corpses were piled high at the end of the day. This did not restore relations with God. After the Levites had accomplished their task, Moses addressed the people. 'You have committed a great sin.' No compromise for the intercessor, but a heart of compassion: '...I will go up to the Lord; perhaps I can make atonement for your sin' (Ex 32:30).

Atonement means at-*one*-ment. Moses wanted reconciliation to take place. Israel's sin was deadly serious and the rebels were incapable of dealing with their sin. Moses' strategy was to ask God to blot him out of God's book so that reconciliation could take place.

'Oh, what a great sin these people have committed! They have made themselves gods of gold. But now, please forgive their sin—but if not, then blot me out of the book you have written' (Ex 32:31–32).

Paul knew something of this intercessory passion and burden. 'I have great sorrow and unceasing anguish in my heart. For I could wish that I myself were cursed and cut off from Christ for the sake of my brothers, those of my own race, the people of Israel' (Rom 9:2–4). Paul's radical statement is, I wish I was cast into hell—if that would bring my countrymen to Jesus and reconcile them to God.

In Moses and Paul we see a radical identification with the people. Are you willing to stand between two worlds to touch heaven on the one hand and a broken, dying world on the other? Will you wield the lethal weapons of intercessory prayer? Are you willing to stand in the gap and be an intercessory change-maker? Will you align yourself with God and allow him to stamp his agenda on your heart? Will you find out what breaks God's heart and pray that it will break your heart too? Are you willing to share in the pain and sufferings of Christ?

John Henry Jowett stated, 'The gospel of a broken heart demands the ministry of bleeding hearts...As soon as we cease to bleed we cease to bless...we can never heal the needs we do not feel. Tearless hearts can never be heralds of his passion.'

Jowett also said, 'To be...in the sacrificial succession,

our sympathy must be a passion, our intercession must be a groaning...and our service must be a martyrdom. In everything there must be a shedding of blood.'

Jeremiah was the weeping prophet. God wants us to experience a measure of that. Blessed are those who mourn in intercessory prayer.

God has called you to be a watchman.

I have posted watchmen on your walls, O Jerusalem; they will never be silent day or night. You who call on the Lord, give yourselves no rest, and give him no rest till he establishes Jerusalem and makes her the praise of the earth (Is 62:6-7).

Certainly, the Lord wants to enjoy fellowship with you and you with him. It was said of that great giant in intercession, Moses: 'The Lord would speak to Moses face to face, as a man speaks with his friend' (Ex 33:11). God wants you to enjoy intimate friendship with him.

God wants you to bring your needs to him in prayer. But he wants you to go beyond that. He wants you to make a commitment to be a watchman. Sometimes God will place a burden in your heart. Sometimes he will plant a desire in your heart to pray for somebody. Follow such promptings, but make a decision—a commitment to be a watchman, to persistently stand in the gap. 'Give yourselves no rest and give him no rest.'

In intercession we are to be like the centurion in Matthew 8. The centurion came to Jesus motivated by compassion. He came 'asking for help' (Mt 8:5), but not for himself. He was concerned about his paralysed servant who was in tremendous pain. Jesus offered to go to the centurion's home and heal his servant. In effect, the soldier said, 'You don't need to do that, Jesus. Just say the word and he will be healed.' He came to Jesus with full confidence in the power and authority of Jesus. Go to it! Come with confidence to the Jesus who declared, 'All authority in heaven and on earth has been given to me'

(Mt 28:18). It is Jesus who is 'the First and the Last'. He lives for ever and holds the keys of death and hell (Rev 1:17–18).

Intercessory agenda

You've made the commitment to stand in the gap. But what kinds of things should you pray for? You will find it very helpful to draw up an intercessory agenda in your prayer notebook. You might find it useful to use the following prayer guidelines.

Pray for your family. If family members don't know Jesus, pray for their conversion. Pray for your non-Christian friends—but how *should* we pray for the unsaved?

Pray for opportunities to share Jesus with them. But that is not enough. Pray for God to send Christians who will share the love of God along their path. But *that's* not enough. Evangelism is not merely communicating a message. It involves setting the prisoners free. It is not by 'might nor by power' but by the activity of the Holy Spirit (Zech 4:6) that people abandon themselves to the lordship of Jesus. Intellectual brilliance or great eloquence won't win the lost. We are totally dependent on God the evangelist, the Holy Spirit, to do his work. Jesus stated, 'No-one can come to me unless the Father who sent me draws him...' (Jn 6:44). We need to pray that the Spirit of God will draw our unconverted friends to Jesus. The Bible tells us that Satan has 'blinded the minds of unbelievers, so that they cannot see the light of the gospel of the glory of Christ, who is the image of God' (2 Cor 4:4). Pray that the Holy Spirit will shatter their spiritual blindness and illuminate their understanding.

When Philip, the bionic evangelist, leaped into the Ethiopian treasurer's speeding chariot, he posed a question. 'Do you understand what you are reading?' (Acts 8:30). The Ethiopian was reading arguably the most

Christ-centred passage in the Old Testament. Isaiah 53 has much to tell us about Jesus and his death and resurrection. However, despite the passage being chock full of information about Jesus, the Ethiopian could not get a handle on it. He couldn't grasp the significance of what was in front of him.

For unregenerate people to embrace the good news, the Holy Spirit must floodlight their understanding supernaturally. Pray accordingly.

Some people—maybe those in your family, or some of your best friends—do not seem remotely interested in enjoying friendship with God. How do you pray? Your prayer for every non-Christian should be that the Holy Spirit will show them their desperate need of Jesus. Pray that the Holy Spirit will convict them of their sin. Pray that he will enable them to see their guilt before God and that they will cry out to be rescued, cleansed and forgiven. Pray John 16:7–11 over them!

You can also pray that God would place a thirst and a searching in their hearts. Pray that they would echo U2's 'I still haven't found what I'm looking for'. Pray that dissatisfaction will set in. It's those who hunger and thirst after righteousness who are filled. Pray that they would begin to question why they are on this planet. The Bible tells us there's pleasure in sin for a short period of time. Pray that the bubble would burst. I have a friend who is a dynamic youth evangelist. A major turning point prior to his conversion came at a party. He looked at all the goings-on around him. He asked the question, 'Is this it? There's got to be more than this.'

We've to pray for those in authority over us. It's a command (1 Tim 2:1–4). You can pray for your boss or school-teachers—they are in authority over you. Pray for those in local and national government. Pray that their decisions reflect God's commitment to peace and justice. Find out who your MP is and pray for that person. Pray for the police force. Pray for their protection, and pray that they would not abuse their position. Find out what is happening locally, nationally and internationally. What are the issues? What is God's perspective on how your councillors are spending the community's money? What are God's views on: the way the health service is being managed; the destruction of his creation for economic gain; abortion; the Poll Tax; the structured racism of South Africa; conflict in Northern Ireland; government regulations on broadcasting; etc? I could go on. You will know how God feels about some issues, eg, the mass murder of unborn children, euphemistically labelled termination of pregnancy. You will know that God hates apartheid. Other issues may require research and reflection before you pray to enforce the will of God. What about government policy on housing? When praying for government, pray for the release of justice.

In prayer, be an advocate for the poor, the oppressed, the downtrodden. Speak up to the Judge of all the earth for the voiceless ones. Pray for the homeless and disenfranchised. Pray for the unemployed. Pray for peace (1 Tim 2:2).

Pray for Christian leaders. Pray that God would deliver them from evil. Pray that they would not fall into temptation but would faithfully pursue Jesus with integrity. Pray for their families. Pray for a hedge of protection around them. Pray that angels would guard them. Pray for those in leadership, that they would be full of the Holy Spirit and enjoy wisdom and power as they exercise their ministries.

Pray for those individuals and ministries who are committed to outreach, mission and evangelism. Pray that God would open doors of opportunity for the ministry of the word. Pray for the supernatural enabling and anointing of the Holy Spirit. Those people and organisations who are investing in the advance of the gospel publish newsletters and prayer letters. Get material like that. Read it. Then, in the light of the needs and requests expressed, pray intelligently.

Jesus calls us to ask Father for a release of workers into the harvest field. Pray that God would raise up prophetic, apostolic, evangelistic, pastoral and Bible teaching ministries. Scotland has a desperate need for evangelists to be raised up. There are few of us about! Pray that God would raise up and anoint those with the gift of communicating the good news in the power of the Spirit, and awakening faith in the lost. We need fishers to pull in the net.

The global missionary needs are devastating. For one thing, there is an imbalance in the deployment of personnel. 90% of the world's missionaries are working with only 10% of the global population. That means nine out of every ten people on the planet have only 10% of the missionary force of the church of Jesus focusing on them. There are one billion Muslims in the world, yet there are more missionaries in Alaska than missionaries to the entire Muslim world. There are more Avon sellers in the USA than Christian missionaries to the whole world. Will you make a difference to that imbalance? Only one out of every seven missionaries is a man. Thank God for the women obedient to the call of Jesus. Pray for male workers to be propelled into the harvest fields.

The needs are tremendous. It took from Noah's time to the year 1850 for the world's population to reach the one billion mark. By the year 2000 there will be six billion people on the planet. More than half the world's population has never heard the gospel. There are 12,000 unreached 'people groups' in the world. Of these groups, 4,000 are Muslim, 2,000 of them Hindu and 1,000 Buddhists. These people groups are culturally and sometimes linguistically distinct groups of people. Jesus commanded us to make disciples of all people groups. There are tremendous signs of God's activity in parts of Africa and Latin

America. The church has grown under tremendous pressure in China in a remarkable way. We can praise God for this. But we have an obligation to plead before the throne. So, saint, will you pray? Will you persistently ask the Lord of the harvest to send workers into the harvest field?

Pray for the suffering church. Throughout the world you have brothers and sisters who are paying a tremendous price for following Jesus. Ministries, such as Open Doors, have been established to help suffering believers. Pray for those who are persecuted, that they would know sustaining grace and physical strength. Many Christians prayed for Charles Bester, a teenage Christian imprisoned in South Africa. He was jailed because he would not honour his conscription into the military. He knew that to do so would mean upholding an unjust system. After serving part of his seven-year sentence he is free. Charles attributes his freedom to prayer power.

Charles Mendes was a missionary to the Hindu principality of Nepal. He was imprisoned. His crime? Preaching Jesus! We prayed for his release. At a concert of prayer in Spring Harvest, the youth programme prayed fervently for Charles Mendes to be freed. One young lad had a picture either of an angel or a soldier (I can't remember which) opening the prison door. Today Charles is a free man.

Others still suffer because of their love for Jesus. I was at the Lausanne 2 Congress in Manila, a conference on world evangelisation. M. Y. Chan shared how he had been imprisoned in a labour camp. As a torture, he was given the task of emptying the cesspool of all the human waste. It was so deep he had to walk into it with a shovel to clear it.

When I was in Poland I met three friends from Romania. They were all young men who paid a price for following Jesus. One lad's father is the pastor of a large church. Attempts had been made on this father's life. The secret police monitored the family's movements. A vehicle drove at the pastor, the wrong way down a one way street, and rammed him. He was hospitalised, and while there another attempt was made on his life.

Plead for the suffering church!

Pray for revival and spiritual awakening. In revival God visits the church and it's like a quick transfer to heaven. It's a work of the Spirit of God who quickens the people of God and draws them back to New Testament Christianity. Winkie Pratney tells us, 'In revival the church dormant becomes the church militant.'[18]

Spiritual awakening takes place among the lost. Pray for a Holy Spirit tidal wave to sweep over the church and to usher the lost into the kingdom. Pray for a divine attack on society. Spend time praying 'down with heaven'. Pray for the life of heaven to penetrate and permeate the church. Pray that God-consciousness would hit your neighbourhood, school, community. You might want to study accounts of revival in Scripture and church history. These will be fuel for your prayers.

Pray for the different countries in the world, using a map. Compile information on the countries you want to pray for. Use Patrick Johnstone's excellent resource book *Operation World*. That way you can pray for a country each day.

Pray for unity and co-operation amongst believers. 'United we stand, divided we fall' is true. Denominationalism dishonours the Lord Jesus, who is the church's Head. Pray that a spirit of co-operation would be evident amongst Christian leaders you know.

Pray for ministries like British Youth For Christ—committed to reaching the 8.25 million young people in the UK who don't know Jesus. They already reach a million of them. Pray for your youth leaders, that God would make them role models of the life of Jesus and have God's strategy for the youth ministry.

The list could go on. Spend time drawing up an intercessory agenda of your own. Make it specific and commit yourself to persistent prayer. Be a bridge!

7

Going by the Book

He was a real sight for sore eyes, if you could actually get hold of him. He had that awkward habit of vanishing into thin air just when you did not want him to. You would have stood a better chance of catching a bar of soap in the rain.

He turned up unannounced in the palace. The hairy happening himself, in the presence of the king, issuing a weather report. A weather report! No, it wasn't the man from the Met Office doing house calls. By no means as pleasing to the eye as Ulrika, he brought the long-range forecast, nonetheless.

'Listen and listen good, your majesty, here is the long-term weather forecast. There will be no rain, no dew, no moisture—nothing for the next few years. No precipitation until I turn the tap back on. Goodnight.'

With that startling announcement he was gone. He had been eyeball to eyeball with the worst king up to that point in the nation's history. God's spokesman had boldly engaged in a close encounter with the number one bad guy in the history of Israel's monarchy.

Ahab had heard the weather report from Elijah. Having dispensed the news that umbrellas were useless, Elijah parked himself in a cave. You might be wondering what all the fuss was about. You might be curious as to why

God's man of the moment closed the water supply. Let me clue you in.

King Ahab married Princess Jez from Phoenicia. The problems began when Jez became Queen Jez and set up home with her brand new hubbie, Ahab. She brought her foreign false gods with her. She introduced Baal worship to the royal family and brought destructive influences not only into the palace but into the nation as well.

Ahab was greatly influenced by his little woman: '...he also married Jezebel...and began to serve Baal and worship him. He set up an altar for Baal in the temple of Baal that he built in Samaria. Ahab also made an Asherah pole and did more to provoke the Lord, the God of Israel, to anger than did all the kings of Israel before him' (1 Kings 16:31–33).

It's very likely that Ahab maintained some level of devotion to YHWH, the true and living God. The possibility that Ahab tried to keep appearances up or attempted to have some kind of commitment to the Lord is evidenced in the young royals. Ahab and Jez produced three kids: Jehoram, Ahaziah and Athaliah. Their names were significant; they meant: 'YHWH is high', 'YHWH has taken hold' and 'YHWH is exalted'. What wonderful names! Maybe Ahab even had a 'Footprints' poster or an embroidered scripture text in each of the rooms.

Elijah's name conveys what real faith and genuine commitment is all about. Elijah means 'YHWH is God'. Elijah's very name was a testimony to the uniqueness, authority and supremacy of the Lord.

As we've discovered, Ahab upset the Lord God in a big way because the Lord will have no rivals for his affections. While Ahab could boast of his brood's lovely names which extolled the majesty of God, he and the missus worshipped Baal. It just wasn't on. Elijah was severely unchuffed about this Baal and YHWH religious mix'n'match. If there was one thing Elijah hated it was compromise. Mix and match is all right for the sweetie counter at Woolies, but it's no way to live before God.

Ahab had followed normal diplomatic policy. If you married a foreigner it was normal for them to continue their religious practices. However, Jezebel's Baal worship was no private religious hobby. She employed a large staff. (In the Carmel close encounter, Elijah made the observation that Baal had 450 prophets.) And Baal worship was the conduit for destructive and depraved practices to flow into the life of Israel. Not only did Baal's demonic worship steal the honour rightfully due to YHWH—that worship involved ritual prostitution and child sacrifices. No wonder the Lord God was displeased.

And no wonder Elijah was upset. God was being insulted; he was not being honoured. Israel was going down the toilet fast. Elijah decided to do something about the desperate state things were in. Elijah prayed!

'Elijah was a man just like us. He prayed earnestly that it would not rain, and it did not rain on the land for three and a half years' (Jas 5:17).

People were locked into the demonic worship of a foreign deity. A wave of immorality and corruption was polluting society. And Elijah prays for a drought. 'Good one, Elijah—that's intelligent praying for you,' you think, sarcastically.

Hold on, though—Elijah knew what he was about. His praying struck right at the heart of Baal worship. Baal was supposed to be the god of fertility who controlled the winter rains. Elijah had thrown the gauntlet down. Notice how Elijah opened up his royal weather report. He began with: 'Since the Lord God of Israel is alive and well...' (see 1 Kings 17:1), and he concluded: 'The water's being switched off.'

Elijah spelt things out very clearly to Ahab. 'King, you are about to see that Baal is useless. Baal does not control the rain or the sky. You are about to discover that the God

I serve is on the throne. Baal worship is a dead loss. Here endeth the lesson.'

If you translated James 5:17 literally, it would say of Elijah: 'With prayer he prayed.' That sounds rather clumsy. It means, Elijah got stuck in there. Elijah spoke to Ahab with great confidence because he no doubt prayed with great confidence.

What was the source of Elijah's holy audacity? Why did he shut the heavens up? Elijah had got hold of a key to effective prayer. This was the key that turned the tap off, and then on, in the space of three and a half years. Elijah prayed in line with the will of God, because Elijah prayed in line with the word of God. God had spoken, and Elijah knew the mind of God.

Note the following scriptures very carefully:

> Be careful, or you will be enticed to turn away and worship other gods and bow down to them. Then the Lord's anger will burn against you, and he will shut the heavens so that it will not rain and the ground will yield no produce, and you will soon perish from the good land the Lord is giving you (Deut 11:16–17).

Further on in Deuteronomy, the consequences of not living in obedience to God are recorded: 'The Lord will strike you...with scorching heat and drought...the sky over your head will be bronze, the ground beneath you iron' (Deut 28:22–23).

God wanted whole-hearted commitment from his people. He would punish spiritual treason. The Baal followers credited Baal as the rain-giving god. If, through sinfulness and stupidity, the Israelites got locked into Baal, they would be confronted with the truth the hard way. Sometimes hard hearts need to learn hard lessons.

When Solomon dedicated the temple he built to God, he prayed. In his prayer he said, amongst other things, 'When the heavens are shut up and there is no rain because your people have sinned against you...' (1 Kings 8:35).

You've checked the Scriptures—are you in the picture? Elijah did not pray for drought because he hated using umbrellas, raincoats and cagoules. Elijah prayed in accordance with the revealed will of God. Elijah prayed by the Book. Here was the basis of his authority. Elijah acted with confidence and prayed boldly because he did so standing upon the clear promises of God.

This is a vital principle for you to latch on to. If you want to pray with authority, go by the Book. Remind God of his promises. Stand firm upon the promises of God. Call God to be faithful to what he has said. God is not a liar. If God says something, he says it because he means it. If it's in the word, it's in his will. Pray with the backing of heaven. 'Be done will of God!'

As the hymn writer, R. Kelso Carter, put it:

Standing on the promises that cannot fail,
When the howling storms of doubt and fear assail.
By the living word of God I shall prevail
Standing on the promises of God.

Get into your Bible and pray the word of God back to God. If you are praying into a specific situation, dig into your Bible for God's verdict. Plunder his promises, use them as prayer fuel. Call God's attention to what he said he would do.

Also, turn your Bible reading into praying the word. Your scripture reading can be a launch pad for praise, adoration, confession or intercession.

You read, 'I am the good shepherd. The good shepherd lays down his life for the sheep' (Jn 10:11). You turn that verse into prayer: 'Lord Jesus, I thank you that you are committed to looking after me just like a shepherd protects his sheep. I praise you for the security of your love and protection. I thank you that you are totally and utterly committed to me. Thank you for laying down your life for me. Because you died for me, I'm accepted and forgiven by Father.'

You come across Mark's account of Jesus healing a leper: 'Filled with compassion, Jesus reached out his hand and touched the man. "I am willing," he said. "Be clean!" Immediately the leprosy left him and he was cured' (Mk 1:41–42).

You mull the verse over in your mind. You begin to chew on different phrases and then pray.

'Lord Jesus, I thank you that your heart is full of love and compassion. I thank you that you love me, but Lord, I recognise that my heart is like a lump of ice. Your compassion motivated that healing. I need your compassion to be operative in me and through me. Melt my heart O God, Amen.'

'Lord, you could have pronounced healing at a distance, but you didn't do that. You touched the leper's rotting flesh. You got up close. Lord, I want to get involved with broken people like you did. For so long I've been distant. Forgive me. I want to be like you. Use me as a channel of your healing. Lord, you didn't need to be coaxed into healing that guy. I praise you that you are Jehovah Rophe—the Lord who heals. You are stronger than sickness and disease. I praise you that you still have power to heal.'

Get the idea?

Use the Bible to determine your prayer agenda. Here are some very useful scriptures for you to use in praying the word over your life and the lives of others. The word of God is a sword; it's your offensive weapon. Wield the sword (Eph 6:17; Heb 4:12). The word of God is powerful and lethal (Rev 1:16, 2:16, 19:15).

When you pray, it is important that you get tuned into the Holy Spirit's wavelength. Pray over your ears that you will clearly hear the voice of God. From God's mouth comes knowledge and understanding (Prov 2:6). Scripture calls you to: 'Apply your heart to instruction and your ears to words of knowledge' (Prov 23:12).

The Bible tells us, 'Ears that hear and eyes that see— the Lord has made them both' (Prov 20:12). So pray that you will hear God's voice, that he will speak clearly into your life as you wait upon him in your prayer closet with an open Bible. Pray over your eyes. Pray that you will see things from God's perspective. Paul prayed that the Ephesian believers would have the eyes of their hearts illuminated (Eph 1:17–18). The psalmist prayed, 'Open my eyes that I might see wonderful things in your law' (Ps 119:18).

I've 'spiritualised' the Bible references to ears and eyes, but you could take them more literally. Every day we hear all kinds of verbal junk: blasphemy, gossip, dirty stories, slanderous suggestions and the like. You may need to pray for cleansing after some of the day's sludge filters in through your ears. You will have to pray over that story that belittled a church leader.

What about your eyes? We are confronted with a deluge of destructive visual images if we indiscriminately sit like couch potatoes in front of the TV. Similarly, the box or the cinema screen offer a parade of pornographic images. The point is: you don't have to drink them in! You could use Job's commitment as a scripture to pray over your life: 'I made a covenant with my eyes not to look lustfully at a girl' (Job 31:1).

Pray the word of God over your mouth. Pray that what comes out of your mouth would please God (see Psalm 19:14). Pray that God would give you self-control in your speech (Ps 141:3). Pray that what comes out of your mouth would be an upbuilding source of life (Prov 10:11,21). You might want to ponder what James says over your speaking (see James 1:19–20; 3:1–12).

You can pray the word of God over your hands (see

Ecclesiastes 9:10; Psalm 24:4; 90:17). Pray for your feet. Pray that God will order your steps (Prov 16:9). Pray that God will give you lovely-looking feet. Yes, beautiful feet! 'How beautiful on the mountains are the feet of those who bring good news, who proclaim peace, who bring good tidings, who proclaim salvation, who say to Zion, "Your God reigns!" ' (Is 52:7).

Read Romans 12:1–2 and make it your daily prayer of surrender that you might be a living sacrifice.

I've given you a few Bible references—don't ignore them. Take the time to read and study the verses I have not quoted. Read the references I've given you and pray them, as appropriate, over your life.

You might want to pray the following verses over your dad or your husband. You might want to pray Malachi 4:6 into your own family.

If you're a guy who's married or moving in that direction, pray some of these scriptures over the love of your life: Proverbs 31:10–31; 14:1; Psalm 127:1.

Paul had a fair bit to say about domestic relationships in Colossians 3 and Ephesians 5. Study what the apostle had to say and pray what is appropriate into your life. We want the Lord to be changing us! Sometimes instead of praying, 'Lord change my wife, my brother, sister, dad, husband, mum...whoever,' we should be crying, 'Oh God, change me!'

If you happen to be a parent or are involved with children, look up these verses, name the children before the Father and pray his word over their lives: Proverbs 23:13; Isaiah 54:13; Malachi 4:6; Luke 2:52; Daniel 1:17.

You should be committed to praying for your church leadership. You might look up the following scriptures: Isaiah 11:2–3; Psalm 75:6–7,10; 90:17; 138:8; 72:15.

As we've already noted more than once, a strong feature of your prayer life should be intercession for the lost. As you stand in the gap pleading for their salvation, are there scriptures you can pray over the lives of our not yet Christian friends, family and colleagues?

Use Matthew 13:14–15 — pray for spiritual understanding for receptive and tenderised hearts. People who do not love and follow Jesus and live under his lordship are spiritually blinded; their understanding is darkened. Use 2 Corinthians 10:3–5 as prayer ammo. Pray using Psalm 107:10,14. Push back the darkness in prayer. I've gone into a little detail on scriptural guidelines for praying for the lost, so I won't labour the point here. Let Scripture formulate and inform your praying.

By the way, some of my material in this chapter on praying Scripture into issues was drawn from a talk I heard at a Youth For Christ staff conference. Cathy Casto from Church on the Rock was the speaker. Credit where credit's due!

8

Standing Together

When Jesus taught us the pattern prayer, he did not have in mind Christians praying in isolation from one another. Jesus' opening words are very significant. We were not taught to pray, 'My Father'. We were taught a prayer framework which opens 'Our Father who is in heaven.' Revd Jim Graham has stated, 'We relate to Christ singularly, but we do not live our Christian lives in isolation.' The poet John Donne stated, 'No man is an island.' This is true of the Christian life.

The Christian life has both an individual and a corporate dimension. If you are Christian you have a personal relationship with the Lord Jesus. You have changed your allegiance, and you are now following King Jesus. In the denomination I grew up in, a 'Christian' song was very popular for a while: 'It's Jesus and me for each tomorrow, for every heartache and every sorrow. I know that I can depend upon my new-found Friend, and so to the end...it's Jesus and me!'

Although the song was popular, in my opinion it's wrong! It promotes individualism. The Christian life does not consist of 'Jesus and me'. If you are a genuine Christian, you are part of a community, you're a member of the body of Christ. You are part of the church of Jesus. The church is not bricks and mortar—it is God's people. If I informed you, 'I am a footballer,' your question in response to this remarkable fact might be, 'What team do you play for, Bill?'

'I don't play for a team.'

'Well, who do you play *with*?'

'Nobody.'

You would rightly conclude from this that I was a wee bit odd. If you play football, you play as part of a team. No matter how brilliant you are, you cannot play on your own. Pelé, Cruyff, Maradona, Gazza, all play (or played) their football as part of a team.

Christianity is a team experience. Down through history God has related to groups of people. In the Old Testament God chose a nation, Israel. When Jesus began his ministry he chose a group of twelve men to be a little community committed to him. The church of Jesus was properly initiated when the Holy Spirit fell on 120 people (see Acts 1—2). When Peter preached his message on the Day of Pentecost there were astonishing results. There were about 3,000 converts who became part of the Christian community. 'Those who accepted his message were baptised, and about three thousand were added to their number that day' (Acts 2:41). Further on we are told: 'And the Lord added to their number daily those who were being saved' (Acts 2:47). Those who were saved did not live out their new-found faith in splendid isolation—they were added to the church.

These early believers each had a dynamic, individual experience of God. However, their relationship with God was outworked in their relationships with those around them. They were committed to their corporate lives together. They met together daily. They ate together in each other's homes. Their interaction with each other was a source of joy. 'They devoted themselves to the apostles' teaching and to the fellowship, to the breaking of bread and to prayer' (Acts 2:42). A feature of the early church's life together was a commitment to pray together. The family of God came together to speak to Father as a regular practice.

In a very real sense, the church was born in a prayer meeting. Jesus had instructed his followers to wait in Jerusalem until they had received 'the Father's promise' (Acts 1:4, TLB) and were endued with supernatural heavenly power. Those that gathered were a praising and worshipping people (see Luke 24:52–53). However, this was not just a praise party. 'They all joined together constantly in prayer' (Acts 1:14). They were committed to persistent prayer. The Amplified Bible conveys their seriousness in prayer: '...they mounted to the upper room where they were indefinitely staying...' (Acts 1:13). They were going to stay put until they got hold of God's blessing.

We can learn two foundational lessons from the 120 folk who were filled with the Holy Spirit at the upper room prayer vigil.

Firstly, the unity of the early Christians was a crucial ingredient in their praying and in their experiencing the power of the Holy Spirit (see Acts 1:14; 2:1). Ten times in the Book of Acts we are told: 'They were of one accord'. Acts 2 reveals a link between spiritual unity and a release of spiritual power. 'They devoted themselves to the apostles' teaching and to the fellowship...' (Acts 2:42) and 'many wonders and miraculous signs were done...' (Acts 2:43). Acts 4:32 again tells about the believers' unity of heart and mind. The very next verse again makes the link between Holy Spirit power and unity: 'With great power the apostles continued to testify...' (Acts 4:33).

'How good and pleasant it is when brothers live together in unity!...For there the Lord bestows his blessing, even life for evermore' (Ps 133:1,3).

If we want our standing together in prayer to be effective, we must be in right relationships with each other.

Corporate prayer is effective if those who pray do so in agreement. It is pretty much a pointless exercise if we don't pray with unity of spirit and unity of purpose. If your church is splintered by competitiveness, or gossip and backbiting, don't be surprised if there is no sense of power in your prayer meetings. You will do well to hit the ceiling, never mind touch heaven, if there is no spiritual cohesion.

Those early believers were not always folk who enjoyed harmony. I'm sure they had to resolve some conflicts before they became the praying force who were all 'with one accord' (Acts 1:14, KJV). Peter and John seemed to rub each other up the wrong way. We can't be sure of the reason why they didn't always get on. John 21:20–21 reveals a relationship problem. Jesus and Peter were in conversation and Peter noticed they were being shadowed by 'the disciple whom Jesus loved'. Peter let John get on his nerves: 'Lord, what about this guy?' Peter had just been informed about what kind of death he would face. He wanted to know what was in store for Johnny boy. Jesus' stark reply was basically, 'Peter, that's none of your concern—you've got to follow me.'

The disciples were in constant competition with each other. They had a hobby—trying to figure out who would be the greatest. This was a source of heated debate and argument (for an example, see Mark 9:33–39). Even after instances where Jesus clearly spelled out the path of suffering that lay ahead of him, the disciples continued to play their power games. And even Mrs Zebedee, James' and John's mum, got in on the act. She wanted her boys to sit on thrones at either side of Jesus in his kingdom (Mt 20:20–28).

Such discord had to be dealt the death blow. Perhaps in the upstairs prayer venue they got things sorted out with each other. At any rate, their hearts were knit together and they prayed together with a singleness of purpose. Here is a key to effective corporate prayer.

We've already touched on the second secret. They were tenacious. They were like pit bull terriers. They had locked onto the promise of the Father (Acts 1:4–5). They were not going to quit until God had fulfilled his promise and poured out the Holy Spirit upon them. As we've already noted, the Amplified Bible conveys this thought: they were staying put 'indefinitely' (Acts 1:13). They had a specific prayer objective in mind: they wanted Jesus to baptise them in the Holy Spirit.

As you scan the Book of Acts you discover that those early believers were committed to standing together in prayer. The crippled beggar in Acts was healed when Peter and John were on their way to a prayer meeting. The upshot of this miraculous healing was Jerusalem was buzzing (Acts 4:16), hundreds of people were converted (Acts 4:4), and Peter and John were hauled before the authorities. On their release they reported the goings-on to the church. In response, the church prayed for holy boldness to declare God's word in the face of opposition and threats. They prayed for God to perform more miraculous signs and wonders. After that prayer meeting, their building was shaken and they were stirred into action. All those who gathered were filled with the Holy Spirit and spoke the word of God boldly. And God spoke to those believers as they gathered for prayer (see Acts 13:1–3).

Those first Christians knew that the prayer meeting was a power-house. They knew God heard them and that he answered prayer. God even organised a jail-break in response to rather feeble, anaemic prayer, as noted in a previous chapter.

For many of us, public prayer get-togethers do not fill us with excitement and anticipation. God wants us to pray with other Jesus followers. But sometimes—or maybe often—the idea of plugging into the prayer meeting seems as thrilling as watching paint dry.

Some people are put off the church prayer meeting because some dear soul decides to orbit the planet in prayer. Fifteen or twenty minutes later touch-down has occurred. Maybe you've been left wondering, 'How can I possibly follow *that?*' You can't string together pious phrases or theological gems, so you decide to sit things out. You watch the hands on the room's clock drag tortuously towards full time. How can you cope?

I want to offer you alternative models of prayer to the traditional prayer meeting. I also want to offer you some prayer pointers that are applicable to whatever kind of prayer setting you may find yourself in.

Often, the problem with the traditional prayer meeting is its domination by the verbose. Those with the gift of gabbery pour forth to God. You can be left feeling inadequate. Involvement in public prayer should be an inviting prospect—not a form of torture. I was brought up in a church family and became a Christian when I was a boy. Back then, I was always baffled by folk who could manage to pray in public. I thought I could never possibly 'aspire to that'. But be reassured—God is not looking for an army of theologians to perform great speeches to him. God is not looking for marathon men either. The reason some folk take so long to pray is: they waffle! The way some people pray you get the impression that they reckon the longer they pray the more likely an angel is to award them a long-service medal. D. L. Moody was to preach at a meeting where someone droned on and on in prayer. Moody announced a hymn: 'We will now sing hymn such and such while our brother finishes his prayer.'

Public prayer is not an invitation to put on a display for the congregation. Neither is it an opportunity to preach. Prayer is talking to God! When I was at Bible college one fellow's opening gambit was, 'Lord, we thank you for the privilege of prayer. Help us to use it properly and to never neglect it.' This was a frequent prayer opener. This was his way of saying to those of us around him: 'Pray!' He wasn't so much talking to God as he was talking to his fellow students and giving us a reminder to pray. If you're asking God for something in prayer, don't feel burdened to explain in great detail the whys and wherefores of your request to the congregation.

If you are planning to attend a prayer group or prayer event, prepare yourself beforehand. If there is opportunity in the structure to share prayer needs, think in advance about what requests, if any, you should make known. Also, spend time in prayer beforehand. Allow some time to wait on God and to listen to him.

If you engage in public prayer, break the sound barrier. Don't mumble—speak out clearly. In public prayer those who pray aloud should be joined by the 'silent partners'. Folk can't agree with you and stand with you in prayer if they cannot hear you. Be brief and specific in prayer. Get to the point—don't be vague. 'God bless all those who preach your word,' is not specific prayer. Use your normal voice. God understands the Rory Bremner style impersonations that go on in prayer meetings, but don't get in on the act. Be natural—be yourself, you cannot be anybody else. While others are praying aloud, listen! That way you can enter into their praying and perhaps springboard into prayer off the back of some of the things they have touched on.

Make sense when you pray. People are fond of asking the Lord, 'Just be with so-and-so.' What does this evangelical cliché mean? If someone is a Christian, God *is* with them—in fact, he is *in* them! The Spirit of God indwells each and every child of God.

If you are leading a prayer group, try to create a relaxed environment. Have a structure and plan to follow. Don't simply decide to go with the flow. What are your prayer aims and objectives? If you have set a time for your prayer meeting, stick to it. Start promptly and finish on time.

If you're the leader, it's your responsibility to specify the prayer topics the group is to address. You might want to devote specific chunks of time to specific issues. 'For the next ten minutes I would like us to focus our praying on the evangelistic concert on Friday. Pray that there will be no hitches on the technical side. Pray that all those who take part will know the power of the Holy Spirit. Let's pray that Jesus is very clearly presented and that many people will make commitments....' To ensure that people stay on track, you could put the prayer issues on an overhead projector. That way, people can remind themselves of the prayer requests and pray through subject by subject.

Give people clear prayer targets. Praying that God will bless the Friday night outreach event is not terribly helpful. Give people something to aim at. 'Bobby is bringing four of his friends from school: Mark, George, Tom and Fred. Let's pray that the outreach event provides Bobby with some clear opportunities to witness to his friends. George's parents have just split up. Let's pray that he would really become aware of the healing love of God and that God is interested in his problems and difficulties.'

If personal requests are going to be shared, encourage people to keep them confidential. If you want to create an open, secure, environment where people can share personal needs, you must protect their confidentiality. It may take time to build up trust and transparency with each other in your prayer group. Violating peoples' confidence will not enhance the process!

Get alongside other people and spend time praying together. When I was an engineering student I got a lot of strength and encouragement from praying with two or three student friends regularly. We would meet in an empty classroom and seek God together.

In the wider context, church prayer meetings foster a sense of family amongst those who pray together. It is very encouraging to be brought to God in prayer by other Christians around you and to hear them approach God on your behalf.

As an evangelist, I desperately need the prayer support of other believers for me, my family and the ministry we engage in. Two instances stick out in my mind where I was deeply encouraged and charged up by the prayers of my home church. One incident was prior to an overseas trip. The pastor led the congregation in prayer on my behalf, placed his hands on me and shared a word from God for me. The other time was prior to my speaking at Spring Harvest. I think everyone who prayed aloud in the prayer meeting prayed for me. I left for the event with a very real sense of being propelled by the prayers of the fellowship.

We will now look at different ways of plugging into the power-house of corporate prayer. But let me first say that I'm not going to offer you an exhaustive list. Some of the ideas will be new to you; others will not be. The key is to be both committed to prayer and creative in prayer. Make use of the resources that are available to enrich and inform your group's praying.

If you've been sent a missionary's prayer letter...don't inflict the whole publication upon the prayer gathering! Read it through first. Highlight key issues and relate them. If your church has a drama group, you might want to get them to dramatise the activities and requests that your supported missionary has communicated.

You can use your dramatists to communicate biblical truths about prayer. The Bible, and/or preaching, should not be slotted in as programme fillers. You may find it helpful to bring an appropriate promise from God's word to bear in an issue you are praying for. Encourage folk in their prayers; stimulate faith by showing what God has to say. But don't just seize an opportunity to waffle.

Make use of maps—and don't limit the use of them to your overseas prayer concerns. I was involved in a town-wide outreach a few years ago. Tony Keast, the local Methodist minister, was in charge of the prayer ministry. Tony made up a number of overhead transparencies from a street map of the local area. Part of his prayer strategy was to pray for specific areas in the community. His prayer meetings ran for a number of weeks in the build-up to the outreach. He had time to go through a number of overhead transparencies and therefore target the community in some detail. Tony would talk us through the particular area we were to focus on. He would mention the streets, schools or places of interest and influence in that area. All of these things were highlighted on the map that was being projected onto a large screen. This was a very helpful way of systematically praying for the area.

Use newspaper cuttings so that people can pray into current affairs. Various cuttings could be shared amongst the group. You can get printed material transferred onto overhead projector slides. Obviously, the printed page does not lend itself to being read easily, but the photos and headlines will definitely help.

Prayer meetings were never intended to be boring tests of human endurance! Don't make them that way.

9

Prayer Concerts

Concerts of prayer are not novel prayer innovations. Revd Dr Nelson Gray is STV's Executive Producer of Religious Programmes. From some work done in his thesis, he passed on to me information about the Kilsyth Revival in 1741-1742. Over 250 years ago there was a proposal to enter into a concert of prayer. This was taken up all over the country. The proposal eventually crossed the Atlantic where it was supported by the revivalist Jonathan Edwards. My friend, Nelson, wrote to me, 'My purpose in attaching the appendix to my thesis was to show how William Carey, a Northamptonshire cobbler and pioneer missionary to India, was influenced by the concert.'

A prayer concert held over 250 years ago was an important factor in William Carey's life. In case you don't know, he is 'the father of Protestant missions'! Revival broke out in Scotland in the 1740s. A group of ministers in the west of Scotland entered into what they called a 'Concert of Prayer, to Promote More Abundant Application to a Duty That is Perpetually Binding—Prayer That Our God's Kingdom May Come, Joined With Praises'. Quite a mouthful if you say it out loud. They had a prayer strategy—people were to gather for intercessory prayer every Saturday and Sunday morning. In addition to this, there was to be a special prayer gathering on the first Tuesday of every quarter.

In 1746 they decided to broaden the impact of their intercession. They invited all the Christians in North America to get involved. The revivalist Jonathan Edwards wanted to get things moving, so he wrote a pamphlet: 'Humble Attempt to Promote Explicit Agreement and Visible Union of God's People in Extraordinary Prayer for the Revival of Religion and the Advancement of Christ's Kingdom on Earth'. That's just the title! Can you imagine what the pamphlet would be like?

The prayer strategy drawn up by ministers in the west of Scotland was aimed at interdenominational, united prayer gatherings. Their two primary prayer objectives were: 'the outpouring of the Holy Spirit upon the churches of Christ', and 'the spread of the gospel in its purity and power throughout the world'. William Carey was part of the answer to the latter. After the prayer movement got going in Scotland, the Americans joined in and Edwards wrote his pamphlet. Edward's pamphlet deeply affected William Carey and a group of Baptist ministers in his area.

The people were also urged to pray for their own church leaders, and they were reminded of the power of prayer: 'God uniformly represents himself in Scripture as a God that hears prayer.... It is in answer of prayer, God usually imparts any special blessing to his people—thus prayer becomes both our duty and our privilege—the Christian's own comfort and progress in holiness—the conversion of sinners; and the encouragement of usefulness of the ministers of Christ, are all powerful inducements to a compliance with this proposal, and as such, are suggested and urged.'

You might have difficulty digesting all the language. What you can't miss is this: they expected their prayers to have an impact. To get stuck into the concert of prayer was at the same time a tremendously exciting privilege and a big responsibility. James Robe from Kilsyth, and the others in Scotland who got involved with him in the concerts, knew they had not developed a new invention.

'The concert for prayer that is...recommended is not a new thing, it has been the practice of pious people in different times and parts of the church, and which God has been pleased to approve by special tokens of his favour.'

What is distinctive about prayer concerts? What makes something a prayer concert? I was involved in a prayer concert in Inverness a few years ago. I decided to wander around and meet some of the local kids at the close of the event. I wanted to know what they thought of the 'prayer concert' and what they had expected to come to. Some of the young people had expected to walk into a concert with a Christian rock band. Although there is praise and worship, a prayer concert is not primarily a musical event. Prayer concerts involve believers coming together to agree in prayer together. Jesus told us, 'if two of you on earth agree about anything you ask for, it will be done for you by my father in heaven' (Mt 18:19). The word translated 'agree' is the Greek word *symphoneo*. It means to sound together or to harmonise. It is translated 'match' in Luke 5:36. We get the word symphony from this Greek word. Do you get the picture? In an orchestra, a variety of different instruments are brought together to produce a harmonious sound. The instruments must agree. A prayer concert is a prayer symphony. The key ingredient is the spiritual foundation of praying together in agreement.

Having said all this, to make a prayer concert happen you need more than a common desire to pray and unity of purpose in prayer. If you, along with some friends, are planning a prayer concert, you might find it useful to look at the prayer concerts I have included here as models to mutilate or build on!

In organising a prayer concert, your aim should be promoting involvement in prayer. You can do this by including a variety of prayer styles and postures and making interaction take place in prayer groups of varying sizes. By shifting people around from one size of group to smaller or larger prayer clusters you break up cliques. The natural thing to do is to gravitate towards your pals or people you feel comfortable with. If you're organising or leading a prayer concert, you should be sensitive, but you want to ensure that people interact in prayer as much as possible and as widely as possible. Sometimes I've encouraged prayer pairs or prayer triplets to be made up of 'people you don't know', or less threateningly, 'people from another fellowship'. (There's always the chance you'll know somebody from another fellowship.)

Prayer posture can be deeply significant and symbolic when we pray together. We can get on our knees together like Paul did in Ephesians 3 to express urgency in prayer. We can get on our knees to say, 'Lord, we humble ourselves in your holy and awesome presence.' You could steer people into a rugby scrum. This can be fun, especially if you discover how powerful your prayer partner's anti-perspirant is! But getting together like rugby players when we pray is an outward sign of our solidarity in prayer. We've come together as brothers and sisters to do business with God in prayer and to unitedly stand together on this issue.

I've used Isaiah 43:5–6 in prayer concerts. I get people to respond physically in prayer to this scripture:

Do not be afraid, for I am with you;
I will bring your children from the east
and gather you from the west.
I will say to the north, 'Give them up!'
and to the south, 'Do not hold them back.'
Bring my sons from afar
and my daughters from the ends of the earth...

I read Isaiah 43:5–6 and get the people to pray for a spiritual harvest, that God might receive spiritual 'sons from afar' and spiritual 'daughters from the ends of the earth'. This isn't done in a vague way. I give people a geographical prayer focus: east, west, north and south. We zero in on a specific area, city or town. So, if the prayer concert is in Glasgow, the prayer target in the north could be Aberdeen. The west could be Belfast, the east could be Edinburgh and the south could be Birmingham. Of course, we could move much wider and pray for the United States in the west, and Germany or Poland in the east. Do you get the picture? Feed your prayer warriors information to facilitate intelligent prayer. So, if your eastern prayer target is Poland you might mention issues like: evangelicals consist of 0.2% of the population; the predominant religion is Roman Catholicism; the nationalism and religion are tied in so that if you're not a Catholic you're not Polish. Get them to act on that information— pray for the countless Catholics, that they may truly experience a living relationship with Jesus.

But—and here's what relates to our discussion on prayer posture—I get everyone to position themselves en masse at an eastern point in the building, then I move them to the west, and so on. I've sometimes encouraged them to pray for an area—together, out loud!

Feel free to move people around your venue for prayer. Movable seats beat immobile pews here. Your venue should be set out in such a way that freedom of movement can take place. If you want people to pick out partners for a prayer triplet, pray together, then double up to form a cluster of six. You'll need to give them room to be mobile. You don't always need chairs! I've been involved in prayer concerts where there were none. People could kneel, stand, lie prostrate or get into a scrum, without negotiating awkward furniture.

Watch the clock! You'll need to think carefully about

the duration of your prayer concert. Decide how long your event will run. If it's 7.30 pm to 9.00 pm, you've got ninety minutes. Think about your structure—time for a brief message, praise and worship, and estimate how long you are going to give people to pray for the various issues you present to them. Time very quickly evaporates in a prayer concert. If people are going to get into a group for prayer, that takes time. They might have to move seats, and/or spy out people to join their prayer cluster. Informing people about what they should pray for and how you want them to pray takes time. Exhorting people on an issue, or reading a scripture to fuel a prayer topic takes time. And you need to allow people time to pray! You will need to keep a tight reign on things. Lost time tends to snowball, particularly if you have a large crowd together for prayer. If you've announced that people have four minutes to pray for the work of Grannies for God in Granton-on-Spey, they shouldn't still be at it ten minutes later!

Write down your prayer concert framework or running order. Allocate a time duration for each item. You are horrified. 'Bill, what if we want to be led by the Holy Spirit?' Well, he can guide and lead you in your preparation before the event! Obviously, we don't want to be put in a strait-jacket—we want to be flexible and pliable and open to the promptings of the Spirit. However, the grand phrase, 'I was led by the Spirit, bro,' can be a pious cover-up for, 'I wasn't prepared, and I managed to fly by the seat of my pants!' You need to bear in mind that younger young people may have informed Mum and Dad that the prayer concert will finish at 9 pm. You're going great guns at 9.45. Dad is at the back of the hall. He might have been impressed if revival had broken out. But Dad is not chuffed. You started late, the praise band slipped in a few extra of their favourite songs, you were not particularly succinct in your introductions, you let things drag on, and hey presto, it's 9.45 pm!

Have a watch with you. Consult your watch and running order while people are on the move or praying. You might find it helpful to have a small team fronting the evening. You can keep each other on schedule. You can discuss what's happening and discern God's voice together, and so on.

You want the people to come together and engage in intercession. However, you can make room for listening to God. If you give people scope to share what God has said to them, you'll need to think of how you can filter this, and communicate it to the group. God might give someone a prophecy to share, or a scripture. In a large group, you can't open it up to Tom, Dick and Harry to share what God has laid on their hearts. Percy thinks he's a prophet—the truth is, he's a balloon. There's a lot of air between Percy's ears, and he enjoys hearing himself generate hot air. You might want to appoint leaders who will weigh up what people feel God has given them to share with the rest of the group. You can discuss with the other leaders what input should be given and when it is appropriate to do so. This works quite well. It gives people scope to share with each other and to exercise their spiritual gifts. This approach safeguards you from the Percys of this world. If someone does not filter through a leader, they cannot have the floor. Even if a prophetic fire is cooking in someone's bones, 'The spirits of prophets are subject to the control of prophets' (1 Cor 14:32).

You will want to allow time for praise and worship. The songs you sing can dovetail in with your prayer themes. Or they can be declarations of prayers that we sing together. We've used Simon and Lorraine Fenner's 'Let your Kingdom Come' as a prayer that we sing together 'in concert'. Songs like, 'The Battle Belongs to the Lord', 'I Will Build my Church', and 'For this purpose' are not only declarations of truth to each other—not just statements of intent or truth to bolster up the saints—they're declarations of war and defeat upon the enemy.

The King Jim Bible renders Psalm 47:1, '...shout to God with a voice of triumph.' You can get people to declare scripture together, or declare war on the Enemy together, as part of your prayer concert, eg, 'May God arise, may his enemies be scattered...' (Ps 68:11), or '...at the name of Jesus every knee should bow...every tongue confess that Jesus Christ is Lord, to the glory of God the Father' (Phil 2:10–11).

I've been in prayer concerts in Glasgow where we've used the city's motto as an out loud, everybody together prayer. Its popular truncated form is: 'Let Glasgow flourish'. However, that is not the motto. The motto is, 'Let Glasgow flourish by the preaching of your word and the praising of your name.'

I might add, don't just use praise and worship songs as programme fillers or musical aids to continuity. Spend some time enjoying God—praising him for who he is and what he has done. Put a voice to your love for God. Verbalise your joy in the Lord. Enthrone him with your praises. God inhabits the praises of his people (Ps 22:3). Praise not only builds faith, but is a weapon to drive back the forces of the Enemy.

You will find the use of audio-visuals a boost to prayer. You can show slides of the area you are praying for. Perhaps you could organise a photographer to take photographs of the schools, young people, arcades, youth clubs, discos and areas where young people hang out in your town. This will be a powerful tool in stimulating prayer for lost young people in your community. You might want to silently show the slides while the people are praying. They can look up at the changing images and pray in response to what they see.

Similarly, you could shoot a video of the areas you will pray for. You could perhaps interview people and discover what Joe Public thinks about the church in the area. You could do a Wogan on why the teenagers doss about in the shopping precinct and then pray accordingly.

A youth worker I know took photos of his area. Drug addiction is a big problem in his area. He took slides of some of the young junkies in his town. He combined his slides with Martyn Joseph's,

> If the children have no hope,
> There is no hope at all.
> If the children have no hope—
> Just their alcohol and dope—
> What have we done?

I ran a prayer concert during the Gulf War. We spent some time praying into the situation. While folk prayed and while I spoke, I had the tea-time news silently shown on large screen video. This provided a powerful visual stimulus to pray. (It also encouraged folk to see the news as a prayer agenda and not just talking heads and information.) Prior to my remarks on the war and encouragement to pray, we showed an excerpt from *Good Morning Vietnam*. The clip we used was the sequence where Louis Armstrong sings, 'What a Wonderful World' while various images revealing the carnage of war flash across the screen. The incongruity of the song and the bloody scenes are very powerful.

I ran a prayer concert where one of our prayer points was the local street team and their outreach to young people in the area. Someone had taken slides of the street team in action, sharing Jesus in the town. In addition, there were various shots of people from the town. The slides were shown while the praise band played and sang 'Such Love'. People were already in their prayer groups, so they moved from the audio-visual straight into a time of intercession.

I've included a couple of prayer concert formats to stimulate your own creative thinking.

I put together a prayer concert for the Mission Scotland Glasgow/Edinburgh Youth Committee. The aim was to get young people praying for God's blessing on the mission meetings. We wanted them to pray for their unsaved friends, and to pray for the evangelist preaching every night, Dr Billy Graham. I worked with Campbell Bell, National Young Adult Advisor for the Church of Scotland.

Campbell arranged the events (one in Edinburgh and one in Glasgow) so that they were on the immediate Sunday prior to the commencement of the stadium meetings in that city. We wanted people to really commit themselves to prayer and personal evangelism during the days ahead. Our hope was that the prayer concert would create prayer momentum.

The event was called 'Down with Heaven'. (In case you wondered, Jesus taught us to pray, 'Down with heaven'— 'Your kingdom come, your will be done, on earth as it is in heaven.')

Down with Heaven

Video	Hammer's 'Pray'	3 minutes
Introduction and explanation of 'Down with Heaven'	Campbell Bell	1 minute
Praise	Stuart Trotter Band	15 minutes

Bill picks up fronting the evening

'Five on the Hot Spot'   5 minutes

Five young people were picked to pray publicly for the following issues:

- that the media opportunities created by the mission would be used by God
- Billy Graham, for physical strength and spiritual power
- that the mission would be a catalyst for ongoing partnership in evangelism
- that God would speak into our lives tonight (ie, 'Down with Heaven')
- a missionary passion would be sparked in young peoples' lives.

Silent prayer individually   1 minute

This was a time for reflection and cleansing (see Psalm 24:3–4) and inviting God to use us during Mission Scotland.

Video: 'Looking in All the Wrong Places'[19]   2 minutes

Prayer triplets   3 minutes

Instruction: 'Pray that God will create a thirst for kingdom life in friends you know who are looking in all the wrong places for purpose, meaning, fulfilment and direction.'

Groups of four   4 minutes

Those gathered were informed that the mission would by and large reach people who had some kind of contact with a church. 80% of those who go forward for counselling at Billy Graham meetings are brought by friends. Six out of seven of those counselled during Luis Palau's Mission to London were part of a church group. (We wanted people to think and pray broadly. We wanted the mission impact to be broadened by our praying. We also wanted people to be challenged by the limitations of the mission and to pray and act accordingly.)

The people were instructed: 'Get on your knees in groups of four to pray for the young people of Scotland.' While on their knees in an attitude of prayer, they were invited to absorb the following information:

- 88% of teenagers in Scotland have no church connection
- there are 7,000 to 13,500 drug injectors in Strathclyde
- we spoke about AIDS in Edinburgh
- we mentioned that the Orange Order and British National Party have been gearing up for major youth recruitment; the latter had targeted Glasgow schools
- homelessness amongst young people.

The groups were then told to pray that God would reveal his love and power to marginalised young people across the land.

Prayer in song: 'Let Your Kingdom Come' 5 minutes

Groups of five

The audience was informed that 60–70% of those who respond to the call to follow Jesus will be young people. In groups of five they were told to share issues that make it difficult for new Christian young people to feel at home in their churches. How could they help?

Discussion 4 minutes

Pray for the integration of new Christians 3 minutes

Rugby sevens scrum 4 minutes

Pray for Billy Graham, that he would know physical strength and the power of God at work in his life.

Video: *God is Close Enough to Touch* 2 minutes

Comment: 'God *is* close enough to touch, but he uses you and me to touch other young people with his love.'

There was a brief exhortation to engage in bridge-building and personal evangelism. Those who came were encouraged to 'seize the day' of evangelistic opportunity that Mission Scotland provided.

Prayer in pairs 3 minutes

'Pray for opportunities to share Jesus with your Operation Andrew contacts/friends.'

Video: *Sleeping Beauty* and *Top Gun* mix. 7 minutes

This sequence consisted of 'Danger Zone' and 'Mighty Wings of Love' being played over the top of a scene from the Disney cartoon classic. It's the scene where Prince Philip is freed from his dungeon prison cell by Princess Aurora's fairy god-mothers. They snap his chains and give him the equipment to take on the evil Malefocent. Philip is given a shield of virtue and a sword of truth. He is informed that, 'With these weapons, righteousness shall triumph over evil.' Philip then wades into hordes of demon-like figures and slays Malefocent who has turned into a dragon. He then makes his way to Sleeping Beauty.

Comment 3 minutes

Comment was made on the supernatural conflict that we are engaged in. Just as Philip was engaged in a battle against supernatural evil, so are we! He had the weaponry to win—so do we. Comment was made on the fact that the battle is won in prayer (see Exodus 17).

Prayer 2 minutes

For boldness and strength in battle. This was a congregational prayer led from the front.

Praise and worship 5 minutes

If you've had your calculator or finger and toes in operation, you'll know this represented a running time of seventy-six minutes—just over an hour and a quarter.

Here's another prayer concert format we used at Spring

Harvest a few years ago. You'll see it's based on the Lord's Prayer. I believe Ian Savory drew up the programme.

Prayer Concert

Theme: the Lord's Prayer, Matthew 6:9–13. The scripture passage was read out.

Celebration/praise   20 minutes

Message: 'How to use the Lord's Prayer'   10–12 minutes

Worship: 'Fatherhood of God'   10 minutes

1. 'Our Father in Heaven'   2 minutes

People on their own in prayer. Concentrate on how God loves us. The way he cares in love and discipline. Galatians 3:26; John 16:27; Luke 15—the prodigal is welcomed.

SONG

2. 'Hallowed be your name'   2 minutes

Groups of four kneeling. John 17:11; Deuteronomy 10:17—the intimacy and awesomeness of God. The groups were encouraged to pray that our government would fear God. They were told to pray for the honour of God's name in the nation.

SONG

3. 'Your kingdom come'   3 minutes

In rugby scrum groups of six. 1 John 3:8—Jesus comes as a warrior with invasion on his mind. 'Your kingdom come' is a battle cry. The church is the agent that brings in the kingdom. They were given national and local issues to pray the kingdom into.

4. 'Your will be done on earth as it is in heaven' 1 minute

All praying out loud together. They were told to pray for
God's will in the nation, focusing on the David Alton bill.

5. 'Give us today our daily bread' 7–8 minutes

God is the giver of good things. The group participated in an
agape meal, sharing pieces of bread with each other. This was
done as a reminder of God's provision and faithfulness. It was
also done to encourage the participants to be the bread of
encouragement to each other and to build each other up.
People spent time praying for each other.

6. 'Forgive us our debts, as we also have forgiven our debtors' 2 minutes

The two minutes was spent with people kneeling on their
own. This prayer time focused on our need of forgiveness,
repentance and breaking the power of cancelled sin. 1 John
3:9; 1 John 1:8.

7. 'Lead us not into temptation, but deliver us from the evil one' 2 minutes

In twos. Prayer focus: that we might know victory over sin,
and that we would be people that flee from sin. Leviticus
20:23,26; Romans 12:1–2.

8. 'For yours is the kingdom and the power and the glory, for ever and ever, amen'

All standing; all shouting out the above. 1 Chronicles 29:10–
13. The event moved into a time of praise, declaring the
achievements of God and the success of his kingdom.

You will notice that much longer could have been spent
praying under 3 or 4. A number of issues could be prayed
for under, 'Your will be done...'. However, you need to

bear in mind the prayer stamina of those you're working with.

For many young people, a prayer concert provides a less daunting forum for prayer than the church prayer meeting. A prayer concert is fast moving, quick changing, interactive and maybe even multi-media! These features make it user friendly. Some folk will take their first faltering steps in public prayer in that framework. You might want to decide what your total praying time target is and then plan your programme accordingly. The first format allowed thirty minutes of actual prayer; the second allowed nineteen.

Despite all that we've said, some people will find a prayer concert a very intimidating prospect. Prayer meetings usually mean spectating—not participating. You can try and put people at ease who are sweating hailstones at the prospect of praying out loud with others. You might announce at the start of the evening, 'We will be engaging in a variety of prayer activities and prayer groups. Don't feel put on the spot. If you don't feel comfortable praying out loud, don't feel pressurised. But we have come together to pray, folks—so do feel free to get stuck right in.'

In a prayer concert, you will often discover that the Holy Spirit puts pressure on people. That's quite another issue. He can turn up the spiritual thermostat and make people aware of the fact that they are not Christians or that there are issues in their lives that need to be dealt with. In a large crowd you can designate a counselling area where people can slip off to for spiritual help. You need to bear this in mind in your preparations. If the Holy Spirit is probing into peoples' lives as God's people pray, you will need some counsellors at the ready. Lots of exciting things happen not only as a result of prayer concerts, but *in* prayer concerts. I've been in prayer concerts where people have been converted, healed and filled with the Holy Spirit!

Dave Bryant has written a superb book, called, *With Concerts of Prayer*. In it, he maintains that the twin focus of prayer concerts should be the renewal of the church and the evangelisation of the world. This is something to bear in mind when organising your prayer concert.

Perhaps you've had the misfortune of being part of a prayer meeting where the prayer agenda has been dominated by someone's gall-stones or ingrown toenails. Obviously, people's physical needs are important, but Jesus never told us to pray for the sick. Jesus told us to heal the sick! Prayer meetings can run down the same old track: 'Lord bless those of our number who are sick. Bless Mr Brown, bless Mrs Green, bless old Mr White, etc. Lord, we lift up our brother before you in his bed of sickness.' I've heard that prayer a few times; it can conjure up quite an image! The one lifting up before the Lord Mr Grunt is six inches smaller and four stone lighter than Mr Grunt. Could anyone lift up Mr Grunt? And there's old Mr Grunt floating in his bed of sickness, enjoying the company of yesterday's lunch!

This says something about our lazy use of language in prayer. But it also highlights the danger of introspective prayer meetings. If we follow Dave Bryant's plan, we will focus on prayer for a mighty outpouring of the Spirit. We will pray for heaven to touch the earth and revival and spiritual awakening to result. We will also 'look out' in prayer. Look out to the lost and dying world around us and engage in intercession. We won't just mark time praying for Mrs Treadmill's bunions.

Make a commitment to focus your prayer concerts and your praying in general on the aim of an open heaven. Pray for revival. Arthur Wallis defined revival as follows: 'In revival the church dormant becomes the church militant.'[20] Revival will affect the community—it may touch a whole city or affect a nation. But revival is a work of God's Spirit amongst God's people. The dying embers of Christians are fanned into flame so that God's people are dominated by a white hot love for Jesus. In revival, the Holy Spirit brings Christians back to 'normal', back to New Testament Christianity. According to *Webster's Dictionary*, revive means 'return, recall, or recovery to life from death or apparent death'. So revival releases life into something that is dead or that appears to be dead. *Webster's* offers the example of the revival of a drowned person. Revival is not for something that never lived. Revival is not for the unregenerate—dead in their trespasses and sins.

Revival is heaven-sent. Arthur Wallis has said revival has two foundation stones: 'the preparedness of man and the sovereignty of God'. God alone sends revival, but we've got to be ready! The great Bible teacher Dr G. Campbell Morgan has said, 'We cannot organise revival, but we can set our sails to catch the wind from heaven when God chooses to blow upon his people once again.' Set your sails; engage in concerted prayer for revival.

I would also urge you to make prayer for the fulfilment of the Great Commission a top priority. If you organise a prayer concert, make that a feature of your prayer agenda. The battle of world evangelisation will be won or lost on the basis of our commitment to pray. S. D. Gordon said, 'Prayer is striking the winning blow, service is gathering the results.'

The truth of Gordon's statement is illustrated in the ministry of Billy Graham. There is no doubt God has uniquely anointed Billy Graham and raised him up to be a reaper. People say they have heard better preachers than the great evangelist. But oratory is not the issue. Homiletical skill is never the issue in evangelism. The Billy Graham Evangelistic Association recognise this. Their motto is Zechariah 4:6 (KJV): 'Not by might, nor by power, but by my spirit, saith the Lord of hosts.' This is why there is a tremendous emphasis on prayer in Billy Graham missions. Thousands of Christians are mobilised to pray. With Operation Andrew, prayer triplets and special prayer gatherings are all set up. Clearly, there are factors other than preaching involved in Billy Graham's fruitfulness as an evangelist. A key must be the enormous prayer backing.

C. H. Spurgeon said, 'Prayer is the slender nerve that moves the muscle of God.' Clearly, we need to see the Almighty flex his muscles—we need to be dedicated to concerted prayer.

10

Prayer Permutations

We've looked at the need to come together to pray together. We've made mention of the church prayer meeting and prayer concerts, and looked at some practical pointers for group prayer. Now, we are going to look at some different prayer models and types of prayer that you can introduce to your corporate praying.

First, we need to remind ourselves again that God seems to put special stock on corporate prayer—Christians praying together. With talk of much-needed revival today, people are fond of quoting 2 Chronicles 7:14:

> ...if my people, who are called by my name, will humble themselves and pray and seek my face and turn from their wicked ways, then will I hear from heaven and will forgive their sin and will heal their land.

The unique power of praying together in agreement is shown in that oft-quoted passage, '...if two of you on earth agree about anything you ask for, it will be done for you by my Father in heaven. For where two or three come together in my name, there am I with them' (Mt 18:19–20). The words of Jesus show us the tremendous value and power in agreeing together in prayer. There are different ways in which we can come together in prayer.

The buddy system

This is a prayer pair consisting of two very close friends. We are talking bosom buddies, not acquaintances. Plan to meet regularly—once a week, say—with your 'buddy'. Since the buddy system stands or falls on the depth of relationship, this will be someone you have a great deal of confidence in. Your buddy is someone you can be open, honest and frank with. You are able to share your heart's desires, hassles, struggles and sins together in confidence. This is likely to be someone you spend a lot of time with. Prayer could flow spontaneously out of the things you do together. However, you might find it helpful to plan a prayer pair time. You could plan half an hour together after school or work or Bible class is finished, or plan to have tea together and pray before you have your meal.

This prayer structure is a Jonathan/David set-up. They had a very deep, intimate, God-given friendship. (You can study this in 1 Samuel 20.) This prayer unit will probably tend to focus on each other's needs and be a source of real strength and encouragement.

Prayer triplets

Prayer triplets came to the fore in the UK during Mission England a few years back. Three Christians get together to pray for three unconverted friends each. That way nine non-Christians are targeted in prayer. There were marvellous stories of people being converted long before the evangelistic meetings took place. God answers prayer! But this seemed largely to be a temporary prayer model which was not pursued a great deal after the mission phase of Mission England had concluded. This was probably due to the fact that it was introduced to people in the context of a specific evangelistic project and was maybe perceived as a run-up technique. I am aware of groups who are still committed to prayer triplets...'And why not?' as Barry Norman might say.

When I joined Youth For Christ, something very exciting was taking place. God was speaking to the leadership and the movement. What was Father saying to us? He was challenging us to be people of prayer. But this was more than a 'Get your house in order, children' belt round the lug. God challenged us to motivate and mobilise young people to pray for revival and spiritual awakening amongst their peers. God had spoken very clearly. However, he continued to put spiritual paraffin on the fire he had begun to kindle.

Rob White, a former Director of BYFC, took a sabbatical, during which he visited Korea and the USA. He visited Dr Paul Yonggi Cho's church where prayer is very much the life-blood of all that goes on. They even bought a mountain so that Christians could hide away in various rooms there and pray. What's more unusual: a mountain with rooms, or prayer being a fellowship's life-blood?

Rob also visited Church on the Rock in Rockwall, Texas. The pastor, Larry Lea, is committed to raising up an army of 300,000 intercessors from across the US to pray for God's kingdom to come in America. Church on the Rock is very much built on a foundation of prayer. I have heard that they have two prayer meetings every week day at 5 am and 6 am, in addition to other prayer ministries. Saturday evenings are devoted to praying in a spiritual harvest during Sunday's services. Church on the Rock also has an all night prayer meeting the first Friday night of every month.

Rob White's sabbatical also involved time drinking in the atmosphere of congregations that throbbed with prayer power.

We also took to the road with 'Going for Glory'. This was a prayer concert which we took around Britain. We did 'Going for Glory' a second time, teaming up with

Youth With A Mission and the Assemblies of God
National Youth Council (now Youth Alive Ministries).
These were evenings of prayer in their own right. But they
also aimed to stir up people to be prayer warriors. Hundreds committed themselves to do so.

Part of the prayer mobilisation strategy was to see
prayer pace-setters emerge, people who not only got hold
of the call to pray but who would encourage their friends
to get on track with prayer, just like the pace-setters at an
athletics event. The pace-setter gets ahead of the rest and
helps the others get moving along at speed. A pace-setter
in a race does not have to be world championship material. Similarly, a prayer pace-setter does not have to be a
cross between Rees Howells and Rambo, or another Praying Hyde—just someone with a heart for God, and a
desire to pray and learn more about prayer, who would set
the pace in prayer. The vision was armies of dangerous
young people in potent clusters across the land, in contact
with heaven and praying down God's blessing in the
church and in the world.

As a result of Rob White's contact with Church on the
Rock, John and Kathy Casto ministered at a BYFC staff
conference. Their visit had a profound effect on my own
prayer life and the praying of my colleagues. I believe God
used their visit to release a spirit of prayer into many
people.

During this time of the trumpet blast to pray, Youth
For Christ International was developing a network of
praying young people that would hopefully span the
globe. (YFC's vision is for a world youth prayer network
of young people committed to extraordinary prayer.) John
Earwicker wrote a document for YFC staff workers on this
vital issue of mobilising young prayer warriors. In it, he
defined extraordinary prayer:

(It) is not concerned simply with personal or localised issues.

It is not concerned with those things which we would like God to do. It is fundamentally about seeking God to accomplish all of his will and plans for the whole church (not just our part of it) and for the whole earth (not just our corner). It is taking God's agenda as revealed in Scripture and asking him to do all that he has promised.

Earwicker continued with a telling comment on extraordinary prayer: 'Usually, our praying isn't that big and selfless. Yet what we are calling extraordinary prayer is really the normal, everyday kind of praying God wants from us.'

People are beginning to respond to what pastor Jack Hayford has called the Holy Spirit's wakey-wakey call to prayer. Trevor Gregory has been involved in developing the prayer ministry in BYFC. As National Prayer Co-ordinator, Trev is involved in training up the prayer troops for battle. In Scotland, God, just in recent years, has raised up ministries with a commitment to prayer and to mobilising prayer warriors. We have seen ministries such as Telephone Prayer Chain, Concern for Scotland, and There is Hope emerge, in addition to other groups such as Lydia Fellowship. That is exciting, but there's more! These groups co-operate and share and pray together. They relate to one another under an umbrella: 'Prayer for Revival Networks, Scotland'.

Why am I telling you all this? To remind you that God has been speaking to his church about prayer. There have been huge prayer gatherings in Birmingham's National Exhibition Centre. Leaders met for prayer there; there was teaching on revival and prayer for revival. The Marches For Jesus have had a strong emphasis not just on parading and praising, but on prayer for the land. God is up to something. He wants you to get in on the action.

The good news is that God is not committed to a 'big is beautiful' philosophy. The Bible says, 'Do not despise this small beginning...' (Zech 4:10, TLB).

There's a gospel song that reminds us, 'Little is much when God is in it.' The human catalysts in the Hebridean revival were two elderly invalid ladies who got hold of God. A prayer pair who touched heaven! There was no town hall packed with eager hordes for a prayer concert. Obviously other folk were crying out to God to pour out his Spirit. But these two sisters in Barvas, both in their eighties—one blind, the other virtually crippled with arthritis—were in tune with God. They prayed down some of heaven onto their little village.

So, you can make a difference—you and your praying friends. Why not form a prayer triplet? 'A cord of three strands is not quickly broken' (Eccles 4:12). You could set the pace and settle a time and a place to get into praying big with a couple of your friends. Or could you be a bit more adventurous and organise your youth group into praying triplets? Set a target of half a dozen triplets.

For such a scheme to work, there's got to be a commitment to make it happen. Set a regular time to meet together, eg, Monday nights at 5.30 pm. Determine how often you'll meet up together—weekly, fornightly, twice a week, or whatever. You are not getting together for a chat, or to listen to your pal's latest CD. You are investing your time together in prayer. Adopt a clear prayer agenda and pursue it vigorously. Know why you are meeting together right from the start.

The triplet is not a bless-up time for the Three Amigos. It's not a 'bless those wonderful missionaries in Bongo-Bongo land, and please heal Aunt Zelda's lumbago' prayer time. Your prayer triplet should be a focused opportunity for specific intercession, not a three-way navel-gazing exercise.

You should pray for each other. But do not get bogged down with praying into your own lives. Pray that the Holy Spirit's fullness would be a reality for each of you. Pray that you would become more and more like Jesus in his beauty, love, power, authority and holiness. Pray 2 Corinthians 3:18 into each other. Pray that you would each become lethal weapons in the hands of God.

Don't stop there! Pray for your unsaved friends. Pray for your whole school or office if you like, but get a narrow focus. Target a handful of your friends and pray them into the kingdom. You will discover that not all of your friends will come sprinting into the kingdom after your first triplet time. They will not all be thrown off their push-bikes by an angelic kickboxer bathed in heavenly floodlights, and yell out, 'What must I do to be saved?' while a dozen angels hum, 'Just as I am.' Conversion *can* be violent and sudden. Coming to Jesus is a crisis experience. You're either dead or alive; living for Jesus, or living for yourself. There has to come a point of decision when you step out of your self-absorbed darkness into the light. However, while conversion is instantaneous, it is also a process.

Take Saul of Tarsus. He had a violent, dramatic Jesus experience. He was literally blinded by the light. He heard a voice from heaven. He was transformed instantaneously. He had been living for himself, a fierce skin-head whose burning ambition in life was to stamp out Christianity. But when Jesus spoke to him, his response was, 'What shall I do, Lord?' (Acts 22:10). He submitted to the authority of Jesus.

Splendid stuff. But Paul's encounter with Jesus was not his first exposure to the truth. God had been making investments in Saul's life.

While Stephen the first martyr for Jesus was being bludgeoned to death by flying boulders, Saul was a spectator. Saul was the official cloakroom attendant. All those robes and stuff would affect your marksmanship. The assassins peeled off their coats and Saul kept an eye on their gear. 'And Saul was there, giving approval to his death' (Acts 8:1). But the bigoted little vampire who enjoyed watching Christian blood flow saw a man who was like his Saviour even in death. That whole incident was a link in the chain pulling Saul out of the dark. Why do I tell you all this? If you want to see your friends, enemies, workmates, classmates, family members, and so on, saved...you will need to apply yourself. You will have to stick it out. It can get discouraging. You pray for your pal. Instead of being transformed into a little Mother Teresa (which is just as well since your friend is a guy), he becomes increasingly switched off when you share Jesus with him. Instead of grabbing the gospel with both hands like a drowning man, he behaves more and more like Freddie Krueger from Elm Street.

If you pray on your own and don't see a lot of visible action taking place in response to your pleading, the temptation is to pack it in. However, in a triplet you can support each other. Spur each other on. When one of you is on a downer, the other two can be a source of strength and encouragement. You can motivate each other to continue the prayer battle. You might want to have three non-Christian friends each that you pray for. Then when you get together, you pray for all nine. This, of course, is the way Mission England triplets worked.

You may operate differently. If you meet in a triplet of your own choosing, the three of you will be fairly close. The chances are if you're at the same school or workplace and do a lot of things together, you will share the same non-Christian friends. So you could pray for non-Christians that all three of you know. Pick five or six not-yet Christians and pray for them—pray for their salvation. Pray for opportunities to share Jesus with them, and support each other in the evangelisation of your peers.

If you come from different churches, you have three fellowships to pray for. Pray that the fellowships experience renewal, and pray for the leadership. If you're all members of the same church, adopt another two churches in your town. Pray God's blessing down on Christians from other groups.

You could pray for your country. Spend time praying for revival and spiritual awakening. Pray for an open heaven over your own nation. Duncan Campbell stated, 'Revival is a community saturated with God.' There's something to get to grips with in your triplet. Cry out to God like the prophet did, 'Oh, that you would rend the heavens and come down, that the mountains would tremble before you!' (Is 64:1).

Pray for your own country, but get global. Adopt a country each, and when you meet pray for the church there, for God's Spirit to move and for the nation's unique needs. Each triplet member could assume responsibility for a specific country. You could be responsible for Romania. So you would find out what is happening there, and what God is doing there. As a result of your investigations, draw up a prayer agenda for your triplet to address. Your two prayer partners will do the same for their adopted countries.

Someone said, 'God wants local Christians in a global context, and global Christians in a local context.' God wants you to get global. He wants you to be a world Christian. He wants you to have a heart to change the world. This will begin to happen as you explore what God is doing on his planet, what the Enemy's tactics are, and in response to these activities engage in extraordinary prayer.

Decide how long your triplet sessions should run for. Allow time for praise, sharing prayer issues, answers to prayer and answers-in-progress. Plot out the use of your time together. You could spend ten minutes on your unsaved friends, the same for your church and country, and another ten minutes praying for your global targets. That's half an hour. Obviously you need to have time to share, research and talk about prayer needs and how God has stepped in in answer to your prayers. However, don't fritter time away by waffling to each other. You don't want to just clinically appear, pray, and then disappear. But you should be business-like. Appoint a mutually agreeable time and a place conducive to uninterrupted prayer, and then let rip!

A telephone prayer chain

You can organise an easily activated prayer force by using willing prayer warriors who have a phone. The system is very simple and can be activated as prayer needs and emergencies arise. If you have eight people who want to be a part of this prayer ministry, organise a prayer sequence:

Youth supporters club

1. John Denver
2. Grandpa Walton
3. Mrs Bloggs
4. Duncan Donut
5. Postman Pat
6. Susie Jones
7. Tracey Chapman
8. Theresa Green

John Denver is at the top of the chain. He co-ordinates the prayer chain. All prayer requests are directed to him. Once he is aware of a prayer need, he phones Grandpa Walton and relays the info. When John rings off, two things happen: Grandpa phones Mrs Bloggs, and John starts praying in response to the request.

Those involved are on stand-by. You might want to establish times when people can access the prayer chain. This will depend on the availability of those participating. It could be 6–9 pm any night. It could be that emergencies can be phoned in at any time. This ministry is open to folk who have a desire to pray. People who know how to open their hearts and mouths to God and know to keep their mouths closed if they've been given classified prayer information. Each member of the chain has a copy of the sequence. So if Duncan Donut can't got hold of Susie he'll phone Tracey. Other chains could feed off the one we've looked at. This is a good move if you've got folk who live a fair distance apart. You can cut down on the phone bills by creating chains within the same dialling code.

Non-urgent requests could be filtered in on a set day, eg, each Wednesday evening. But the real beauty of the system is it can be activated when you need it.

You're out pounding the pavement with the local evangelistic street team. You spy a group of unsuspecting pagans. In no time at all you're into a great conversation about the Lord Jesus. Half an hour passes. By this time things are hotting up. It turns out you've got the following congregation on the street: a backslider who packed it all in because someone really hurt them in the church; a very aggressive, verbally abusive sumo wrestler type; a raving demoniac; a totally bored girl doing a good impression of a zombie; a staunch Catholic kid who reckons Rome's the only way to fly; and a girl who's drinking in every single word you say with watery eyes. What do you do? One of your Holy Ghost Rambos slips away from the action and quickly makes his way into a secluded telephone booth.

He emerges looking different; a red cape flutters in the breeze. A crimson pair of Y-fronts are sported. Beneath them, a fetching pair of tights. A large 'S' is displayed on his chest for he is indeed 'Saved'. Clutching a large black Bible in one hand and holding a *Journey Into Life* in the other, he strides purposefully back in the direction of your group. With X-ray vision he pierces the hearts of the unregenerate and then utters encyclopaedic words of knowledge in precise biographical details. Demons are sent sprawling back into the pit at the very sight of this mighty anointed warrior. It's the one whom hell loves to hate. You have been joined by: Super-Christian. The hero of the youth group. Evangelist par excellence. How can those six kids you contacted resist the charisma of the caped crusader?

No, something far more dynamic has taken place. There isn't the drama, nor the spectacle, of Super-Christian vaulting skyscrapers and winning souls. But the atmosphere where you stand is beginning to change. The invisible realm is being affected. Why? Your teenage mutant street evangelist has activated the prayer chain. Denver has been informed of what's taking place, and been given specific instructions to carry out back at mission control. Within fifteen minutes of your street team member slipping out of the phone booth, eight Christians are pouring out their hearts to God.

The loudmouth with a PhD in obscenity has quietened down, and Pamela, the watery-eyed girl, has begun to open up to Christine from your group. Pamela and Christine have moved a discreet distance from the others, and Pamela begins to stumble towards Jesus.

A telephone prayer chain can be a vital life-line between you and heaven. Why not start one?

Prayer walks

I've already mentioned prayer walking as a solo activity. No, it's not something Michael Jackson does—that's moonwalking! A prayer walk can be an exciting group activity.

I've had groups come to Greenock, Scotland, from a church in Seattle, USA. The first group that came was a youth choir, ninety-strong. They did a Rock-Gospel-meets-Kids-From-Fame-style choreographed musical presentation. A much smaller group returned. This second group did street theatre, schools presentations and street witnessing. The group, from Westgate Chapel, were hot on prayer walks. They would get into the town and wander around praying for Greenock, praying in response to the things they saw and the people they met.

You can bunch off in little groups and pray over different areas. Or you can walk together as a group, quietly praying to God for your community. This way you get a 'feel' for the atmosphere in the street. You can plan a prayer route. Take your group into strategic areas in the community and let what they see and hear fuel their intercession.

If you are going out at night, your shopping precinct will be virtually dead. That gives you the opportunity to be very vocal in your praying. However, you will find it helpful to move through the community when people are going about their normal business. Mothers laden with groceries trying to steer their kids down the busy high street; yuppies posing with their vodafones; unemployed kids sprawled on the pavement, bored half to death; old people shuffling to the shops.

You can target key places on your walk. Stop at these locations and pray. You could prayer walk past the police station, the town hall, the high schools, the mosque, the disco, local churches, pubs, cinema.

During a couple of outreaches I've been involved in, we took to vantage points where we could see the whole town. One time I was taking a Christian group into a school. It was the first time such a thing had been allowed. A few of us went to a golf course. From a hill on the course, we could see the school and a fair amount of the town too.

When Westgate visited the Inverclyde area for the second time, we did a bit of praying 'on location'. One of our prayer walks...we drove to! We climbed up a hill, and from there we could see a fair sweep of the area. Then we engaged in intercession for the community.

John Dawson has written a superb book, *Taking Our*

Cities For God. Read it for some encouraging stories that underscore the value of getting prayer out into the street.[21]

Into the night

You could organise prayer activities that run through the whole night, or have a half night of prayer. This half night of prayer could run from 10 pm—2 am. A night of prayer could kick off at 10 pm or midnight, and conclude with a 6am or 7 am breakfast. Such an event might seem an impossibility to you. 'Pray for four hours or six hours, or even longer? You must be kidding!'

The secret is to run through an organised programme and a specified running order and sequence of events. Build in time for praise and worship, coffee breaks, loo breaks, a preach or two, and maybe a video on prayer or an issue you're praying into. You can build in a late night prayer walk if you wish. Organise your event into blocks of time devoted to prayer. The time will move fairly quickly if you are well prepared. If you've been involved in a prayer concert, you will know that it is a fast-moving activity. A well-oiled, well-led prayer concert does not grind along—it speeds along! Three hours could easily be spent in two prayer concerts slotted at either end of your event!

Let's look at a possible running order for a night of prayer which kicks off at midnight and runs until 7 am.

midnight	Arrival and coffee
0015	Welcome and introductions
0020	Praise and worship
0050	Talk on the power of prayer
0120	Prayer for unsaved friends and family
0200	Toilet break
0215	Prayer concert: 'Changing God's World'
0400	Coffee
0420	Talk: 'Will God send revival?'

0445	Toilet break and leg stretch
0500	Prayer for revival in the local churches of your community
0530	Prayer walk around the town
0630	Return to church for praise party
0700	Breakfast and home

I've deliberately not bored you with great detail. We've already looked at putting together a prayer concert. You might discover that you will need more frequent breaks as you progress into the wee hours. It's not unlikely that some folk will nod off. That's all right. The secret is to put together a varied, fast-moving programme that promotes participation.

Drawing out the reluctant

If someone has a desire to pray, light the blue touch-paper and stand back and enjoy the spiritual fireworks. If your participants are keen, all you need to do is provide a structure for them to do the business in. What about those who put public prayer participation on a par with root canal treatment or Chinese water torture? (In other words, very painful and to be avoided at all costs.)

Some people don't pray aloud in prayer gatherings because of a lack of confidence caused by the intimidating presence of those dictionaries with legs who love dominating the proceedings. You can muffle the verbose! Introduce sentence prayers. Not chapters or even paragraphs—simple, precise sentences. Therefore, a prayer praise time becomes:

'Lord, I love you. You're so patient with me.'

'Yes, thank you, Lord, that you never write us off.'

'Father, thank you for giving us Jesus.'

'Thank you that Jesus took what we deserve.'

'Father, we praise you that Jesus is not dead. You raised your Son from death and hell.'

'Lord, thank you that my mum is out of hospital.'

'Yeah, Lord, thank you that Mrs White's surgery was successful.'

Get the idea?

Similarly, intercession is a brief and to the point exercise for the individuals who participate. You are praying for Bob's pal Tommy who isn't a Christian:

'Father, use Bob to reveal Jesus' love to Tommy.'

'Yes, Jesus, I ask that when Tommy spends time with Bob, he'll be reminded a little bit of you.'

'Father God, release your Spirit with convicting power into Tommy's life.'

'Lord, I ask that Tommy would recognise that he is lost without you.'

'Give Bob the opportunities and the courage to speak up for you.'

Praying a sentence is far less intimidating for a bashful person. You could go round a circle a couple of times, or invite people to chip in as freely as they like. I've sometimes used a pass-the-parcel approach to prayer. You get a book or a Bible and pass it to someone who prays briefly then passes it to the next person, and so on. If someone doesn't want to participate they pass the parcel.

Some of these prayer models might be of real value to you. You might have some great prayer strategy ticking away inside you ready to explode into intercessory action. You might want to adapt some of the things I've shared. The list is not an encyclopaedia of prayer activities, but it should give you some ideas. The point is: get praying. Get alongside a friend, a couple of pals or a group large or small, and move out into the adventure of life-changing, history-shifting, planet-impacting prayer.

Whether your strategy involves prayer triplets, or toast, tea and prayer with young people from right across the church spectrum who love Jesus and who can open their eyes at 6.30 pm, commit yourself to pray and get alongside others who want to learn how to pray.

The early morning prayer meeting is a great vehicle for starting the day at God's throne with other Christians. I know of one church that has a 644 Squadron. No, it's not their own private air force. They meet at 6.44 am, have a continental breakfast and meet with God together. Norwich YFC are not as elaborate—they offer toast! But the main course is the same: intercession. The early morning prayer vigil offers the possibility of folks dropping in, as they are able, on their way to school or work. It has the advantage of giving people a group setting to meet God before they meet the demands of the day. Some of the day's activities can be supported by other believers in prayer. Of course, you could meet in the evening, but as one Irish friend said to me, 'Why put your armour on before you go to bed?'

You might also want to try the following prayer practices:

- Letters to God. Get your group to write a letter to the Lord, perhaps in response to a passage of Scripture.

- Prayer consequences. Particularly for schools work, Richard Morris suggests developing a prayer flow chart where you map out diagrammatically how God steps in and what happens when you pray.

- Liturgy. Anglicans and Episcopalians won't need convincing here, but Richard suggests developing your own, for example for exam time, or the end of term.

11

Battleground

Prayer can be a tremendous struggle. I'm not just saying that getting down to prayer is a struggle. Prayer itself can be a painfully difficult business. God deals with us, gets hold of us and changes us as we pray. This can be painful. The heavenly surgeon wields his scalpel and deals with areas in our lives that are displeasing to him and destructive for us.

Jake found prayer to be a difficult affair. His name was changed as a result of an all-night prayer encounter. He was no longer Jacob; he was Israel, which means 'he struggled with God'. He walked with a limp because his hip was damaged. Apparently, what took place in Genesis 32 was a theophany—an appearance of the pre-incarnate Son of God. Jacob was convinced that he saw God face to face (Gen 32:30). This 'angel' refused to disclose its name to Jacob. Whether or not your theology encompasses theophanies, Jacob found his through-the-night wrestling match with his heavenly visitor a costly business.

Hannah was a woman who got the thumbs-down from the gynaecologist. 'No kids for you I'm afraid, Mrs Elkanah.' She did not ask for a second opinion. Neither did she accept what the medical records coldly stated. Hannah prayed. Her praying was no hallelujah, hand clapping, let's get happy, 'name it and claim it' business.

Her praying involved great pain. '...Hannah wept much and prayed to the Lord' (1 Sam 1:10).

A religious leader accused her of having had a few too many when he saw Hannah praying. How did she respond to this accusation? 'I have not been drinking wine or beer; I was pouring out my soul to the Lord...I have been praying here out of my great anguish and grief' (1 Sam 1:15–16).

The writer to the Hebrews gives us a snapshot of Jesus in prayer. We are told that Jesus 'offered up prayers and petitions with loud cries and tears...' (Heb 5:7).

If you are committed to becoming a bridge—standing in the gap as an intercessor—you will find yourself sharing in Jesus' pain and suffering for a dying world. If you ask God to break your heart with the things that cause his heart to break, you will identify in some measure with Paul's testimony. Paul said, '...the sufferings of Christ flow over into our lives...' (2 Cor 1:5).

Following Jesus does not cocoon you from pain, suffering and difficulty. Prayer does not always involve hovering in the ozone layer, basking in heaven's sunshine with a heart bubbling with joy.

As you get to grips with God in prayer, you very soon discover that prayer involves spiritual conflict. Prayer is a battleground. Prayer is an arena for spiritual conflict. Daniel knew this. Daniel came up against supernatural resistance to his prayers. For three whole weeks he experienced demonic opposition to his praying. Here's a prayer warrior's testimony of life in the trenches:

But for twenty-one days the mighty Evil Spirit who overrules the kingdom of Persia blocked my way. Then Michael, one of the top officers of the heavenly army, came to help me, so that I was able to break through these spirit rulers of Persia (Dan 10:13, TLB).

We have looked at areas where our prayer can get

bogged down. We have explored ways out of dead-end praying. We also need to be clear on the fact that prayer can be difficult and draining because it involves warfare. Prayer means waging war. If you pray, 'Down with heaven! Come, kingdom of God! Be done, perfect will of God!', the hosts of hell will not always sit back and happily see God's kingdom advance.

Christianity is a violent business. Jesus said, '...the kingdom of heaven has been forcefully advancing, and forceful men lay hold of it' (Mt 11:12).

Paul reminds us very clearly that there's a war on: 'For our struggle is not against flesh and blood, but against the rulers, against the authorities, against the powers of this dark world and against the spiritual forces of evil in the heavenly realms' (Eph 6:12).

How can we win through in the conflict? As we march into the arena on our knees, how can we be winners?

Joe Louis was a champion boxer with a remarkable record. He fought seventy-one fights and lost only one. He had twenty-five successful championship defences. He was once asked the inevitable question, 'What's your secret, champ?'

Louis' response was, 'I study my opponent so I'm never surprised, and I stay on the offensive.' We would do well to take a leaf out of Louis' book. Know your Enemy and stay on the offensive!

The apostle Paul knew his opponent. He could say, '...we are not unaware of [Satan's] schemes' (2 Cor 2:11).

When it comes to Satan and the demonic, we can fall into two traps. We can either take the Enemy too seriously, or not seriously enough. Sometimes Christians can almost fall into the trap of dualism (ie, that there are two gods): a good 'un and a baddie. It's a bit like a cosmic wrestling match where we're not too sure of the outcome: 'In the blue corner, the God and Father of our Lord Jesus

Christ, and in the red corner (boo, hiss)...Satan.' Let's have none of it!

We need to be very clear on this: Satan is a created being, a fallen angel. He can only be in one place at one time. He is not like God who is omnipotent (all powerful), omnipresent (present everywhere) and omniscient (all knowing).

Revelation 2:13 talks about Satan's pad—he can only hang out in one place at one time. He is in no way God's opposite number. He is very powerful and absolutely evil, but when Satan got the heave-ho out of heaven, God did not get up off his throne to remove the Evil One. The archangel Michael had the job of celestial bouncer and ejected heaven's former worship leader.

Some Christians take the demonic far too seriously. Some clogged up granny sneezes at the prayer meeting, and before you can say, *'Ghostbusters!'*, five raving charismaniacs are attempting to cast out a spirit of influenza. The cornflakes go scattering across the table, followed swiftly by a tidal wave of cow juice. Was it due to clumsiness and lack of sleep? Oh no! Our cuddly charismaniac bellows across the kitchen, 'Spirit of Kelloggs—I bind you!' Some folk seem to spot demons in every nook and cranny. It is helpful to remind ourselves that God has his angels. There is a heavenly army of God's secret agents. They could outnumber the fallen angels two-to-one (see Revelation 12:4).

Dualism dishonours the living God. 'Hear O Israel, the Lord your God is one God,' is what a Jewish man would chant as he hopped out of bed. Demon spotting gives the Enemy too much credit.

Smith Wigglesworth was a remarkable man of God who had a powerful healing ministry. He once was preaching, firing on all four cylinders, when he fell out of the pulpit. He continued to preach in mid-air. When he landed on his feet he zig-zagged down the aisle like some kind of crazed windmill. He fell on a sick person who had come to the meeting looking for a touch from God. When Wigglesworth landed on them, they were healed! Wigglesworth is reported to have raised several people from the dead! He never claimed to be an evangelist, but hundreds were converted through his dynamic ministry. One day Wigglesworth was woken by a visitor perched at the foot of his bed. It was the devil! Wigglesworth looked up, realised who it was and exclaimed, 'Oh, it's only you.' He then rolled over and went back to sleep!

Smith Wigglesworth lived in the good of the apostle John's declaration to us: 'You, dear children, are from God and have overcome them, because the one who is in you is greater than the one who is in the world' (1 Jn 4:4).

That's the good news! We'll explore the implications of Jesus' cosmic victory over the powers of darkness a bit later on. That is not in question. Jesus is the champion over evil—undisputed King of kings and Lord of lords.

However, the Bible still describes Satan as a roaring lion, on the prowl. We cannot afford to ignore or dismiss Satan. He is not a little guy in a red suit, sporting a beard and brandishing a garden fork as his tail sways from side to side. He is not a cartoon character. Paul's policy should be ours too: 'For we are not unaware of [Satan's] schemes.' Get to know the Enemy's tactics. He uses the same old artillery time and time again.

The Linda Rondstadt syndrome

Back in 1975, the luscious Linda Rondstadt had a hit with a song containing the line, 'You're no good, you're no good, you're no good—baby—you're no good.' It's one of Satan's all-time top ten hits. He loves to serenade Christians with that one, piping the song into believers' hearts and minds. One of the Enemy's titles is 'the accuser'. He delights in telling you you're worthless and useless. You can see him trying to use this weapon in the presence of God in Job 1. God informs Satan about the integrity of Job. Satan responds with, 'Job's only in it for the things you give him.'

Nehemiah was on a God-given project. He had to cope with enemy accusation. 'Your material's useless, your workmanship is garbage—what you are doing won't last' (see Nehemiah 4:1ff).

The Enemy likes to tell you that you won't amount to anything because you are junk. He also fine-tunes his accusations and accesses your memory banks. He whispers, 'You did that? How can you expect God to love you when you did that?' Or when you blow it and then claim God's forgiveness, there's a subtle change of tune: 'Call yourself a Christian? How could you have done that if you are a Christian? How can you possibly claim to love God when you got into that?'

I had been on an evangelistic mission for three whole weeks, and away from the family a bit longer. I decided that rather than take ages on the train, I would buy a stand-by ticket and fly home. I was, however, confronted by a problem. Somehow, quite mysteriously, my suitcase had shrunk. All the things that had sat ever so nicely in place when Morag packed my clothes just would not fit in! My generous hosts came to my rescue and gave me a rucksack and a hold-all. I decided to stash all my dirty laundry in the rucksack. I managed the juggling act of luggage-carrying all the way to the airport. I juggled my way to the departure lounge. My balancing act was interrupted by airport security.

'I'd like to examine your rucksack, sir.'

'No, you wouldn't.'

'Yes, I would ... *sir*.'

'No, you wouldn't.'

'Yes ... *I WOULD*.'

The pantomime ended. I lost the debate. There,

paraded in full view of the great British public, were my sweaty shirts and my collection of dirty underpants, dirty socks and smelly pyjamas.

Satan delights in grabbing the dirty laundry of our past and waving it at us defiantly. He loves ransacking our memory banks, rummaging through our past and subjecting us to repeat showings of our failures in gory technicolor. My friend, Jeff Lucas, calls this 'the video syndrome'.

Satan loves it when we get bogged down in condemnation. Condemnation will foil effective prayer, strip us of our confidence in approaching Father and rob us of our sense of sonship and acceptance.

The Enemy enjoys hitting you with condemnation. But—get hold of this! If you are forgiven there is no ground for accusation. Therefore, 'there is now no condemnation for those who are in Christ Jesus...' (Rom 8:1). 'If we confess our sins, he is faithful and just and will forgive us our sins and purify us from all unrighteousness' (1 Jn 1:9).

The story goes that Martin Luther was minding his own business when he was confronted by Satan. Satan had brought the Reformation hero a present. What was the unexpected visitor carrying? A huge printout of all of Luther's sins. What did Luther do when confronted with these accusations? Cower in a corner? No—he got his pen and began to write across that list. Time and time again Luther wrote, '...the blood of Jesus, his Son, purifies us from all sin' (1 Jn 1:7).

There's a big difference between condemnation and conviction. The Holy Spirit will convict us of sin—that's a different matter. He will single out specific areas to repent of and claim cleansing for in order that we might be drawn closer to Jesus.

But the accuser wants to drive a wedge between you and God. His weapons include the thought bombs of false guilt. As Jack Hayford reminds us, 'The next time Satan reminds you of your past—remind him of his future!' Get the picture? Sulphur soup!

The Fleetwood Mac complex

'Tell me lies, tell me sweet little lies.' This is from a Fleetwood Mac song. And Satan is happy to oblige—he is, after all, the father of lies. Jesus said, '...you will know the truth, and the truth will set you free' (Jn 8:32). Satan does not want you to enjoy such liberty. He wants you wrapped in a web of lies—lies about your God and Father, and lies about you and God's purposes in your life.

The Bible records severe cases of the Fleetwood Mac complex—people who had swallowed lies about themselves. People like Gideon, Jeremiah or Timothy.

Gideon was convinced he was useless. He was a paid-up member of Wimps Anonymous. Gideon would never go near a beach for fear that some macho muscle machine in a pair of too-tight Speedos would kick sand in his face. Gideon had bought into 'worm theology' ('I am only a worm before you, Lord'). Take a look at Judges 6:15. He had difficulty swallowing the angelic salutation, 'The Lord is with you, mighty warrior' (Judg 6:12).

Jeremiah, it seems, thought his youth disqualified him from productivity in the kingdom of God. That's why God steps in and says, 'Hold on there, Jerry. Don't say, "I'm just a little lad"' (Jer 1:17).

And Timothy seemed to have bought into people's put-downs (see 1 Tim 4:12). We can fall into that trap: 'I'm so young. I am so insignificant. God probably can't be bothered listening to my prayers. I'd better not bother God with this issue.' ('Tell me lies, tell me sweet little lies', plays quietly in the background.) If prayer is to be effective, it must spring from a right understanding of who God is and who we are in Christ.

It's important that we don't give the Enemy a foothold. I think it was Robert Murray McCheyne who said, 'A holy man or woman is an awesome weapon in the hand of God.' We must be committed to living lives of integrity and holiness. There is power in purity. When it comes to prayer, this is particularly so.

As Joe Louis, that gloved warrior of a bygone era, reminded us, 'Stay on the offensive.'

You need to be properly clothed and armed. Make use of your heavenly weapons and exercise a singleness of purpose in the battlefield. 'An enlisted soldier does not get caught up in civilian affairs.'

Paul exhorts us (it's 'us' because spiritual warfare is not the terrain of lone Rambos—we wage war together): '...be strong in the Lord, and in the power of his might' (Eph 6:10, KJV). There's a clear need to be filled with the Holy Spirit (Eph 5:18) if we are going to experience the power of God's might.

Buckle the belt of truth (Eph 6:14). I believe this means that the prayer warrior should be a man or woman of integrity. But I think it means, live and pray according to the truth—not your emotions. Reaffirm the truth about God and yourself as you pray.

Put on the breastplate of righteousness (Eph 6:14). You can stand against the Enemy because you have been right-eous-ified by the blood of Jesus. You don't stand on your own merits. Your righteousness is as filthy rags, but you are praying to Jehovah Tsidkenu, the Lord who is your righteousness. *You* are the righteousness of God (see 2 Corinthians 5:21).

Get your footwear on (Eph 6:15). '...your feet fitted with the readiness that comes from the gospel of peace.' Be prepared! A Roman soldier was sure-footed in battle. He was able to enjoy mobility even on slippery surfaces, because not only were his sandals strapped on to his legs, he had spikes. He could move! Likewise, we've got to be in that state of readiness to move swiftly at the Lord's command.

Take hold of the shield of faith (Eph 6:16) which acts like a fire extinguisher when the Enemy attacks you. The helmet of salvation (Eph 6:17) offers protection for your mind. It guards you against Satan with God's supernatural peace that protects the mind (see Isaiah 26:3). Receive the mind of Christ; ask God that you might view things from heaven's perspective.

Take hold of the sword of the Spirit (Eph 6:17). Make use of it. The sword of the Spirit is the *rhema* of God. This is a specific word from God. It could be a scripture that is activated in your memory banks for this specific situation. The clear implication is: soak yourself in Scripture. When Jesus was engaged in hand-to-hand combat with the Enemy in the desert, he used the word of God. Jesus, fully human—the Proper Man, as Luther called him[22]—took on Satan with the same weaponry you have at your disposal. Jesus put the Enemy to flight with the word of God.

Paul also tells us to 'pray in the Spirit on all occasions' (Eph 6:18). We've already looked at the ministry of the Spirit in our praying. Allow him to pray through you. If you have a prayer language, let 'er rip!

As you engage in prayer combat, it is absolutely vital you have a correct perception of Jesus. C. S. Lewis knew that Jesus is dangerous. In his *Narnia Chronicles*, Aslan is 'good and terrible'. Jesus asked his disciples, 'Who do men say that I am?' In reply, he got the latest opinion polls. Jesus then asked his followers, 'Who do *you* say that I am?' This is the key. The 'Who is Jesus?' question came before a summons to discipleship. Our understanding of Jesus shapes our Christian life, the quality of our discipleship and our effectiveness in spiritual conflict.

Take a look at Revelation 19:11–16. You won't find 'gentle Jesus meek and mild'. It is probably the most aggressive picture of Jesus in the Bible. He is a militant warrior King executing judgement on the enemies of heaven's kingdom.

He rides a white horse because he is victorious. Conquering military leaders would return from battle on a white horse. Jesus is Jehovah Nissi—the Lord our Victory. Jesus is our heavenly Joshua. (They hold the same name: Yeshua, meaning the Lord is salvation, deliverance, God to the rescue.) The Old Testament military campaigner took the land and destroyed the authority in the land. Jesus has taken the land and invites us to move in.

It is Jesus who lives for ever. It is Jesus who holds the keys of death and hell.

Boxers like to enter the ring wearing robes proclaiming who they are. Here in Revelation 19 we find that Jesus, our Supreme Champion, has his title not only embroidered and emblazoned on his robe, but tattooed on his thigh. He is King of kings and Lord of lords.

Jesus is 'Faithful and True' (Rev 19:11). He is absolutely trustworthy. Out of his mouth comes a sharp sword—it is the authority of his word that secures victory. His eyes are like blazing fires—he is all-seeing and all-knowing.

We are also told that he has a 'name written on him that no one knows but he himself'. Here is an element of mystery. Jesus is far greater than we can ever hope to fathom. It was also thought that if you knew someone's name you held some kind of power over them. Clearly, the message is: Jesus is unbeatable. He wears 'many crowns'. He is King of every nation and Lord of all.

Perhaps the key verse in this apocalyptic vision of Jesus is Revelation 19:13: 'He is dressed in a robe dipped in blood...'.

The blood of Jesus has secured victory over the Enemy. 'And having disarmed the powers and authorities, he made a public spectacle of them, triumphing over them by the cross' (Col 2:15).

Final victory is secure. In Revelation Jesus is referred to as a lion only once. He is referred to as the Lamb twenty-nine times. He is our Passover Lamb. If you dig into the Old Testament you'll discover that Pharaoh was a stubborn old beggar. Frogs, gnats, water into blood—you name it, like an old donkey he wouldn't budge. The final plague, however, got results. The firstborn throughout Egypt were struck dead. However, provision was made for God's people. If they killed a perfect lamb and daubed its blood on the doorposts, the angel of death would 'pass over'. Get it? There was security under the blood and shelter from the angel of death. We enjoy security and shelter from destructive attacks under the blood. Jesus has conquered the last enemy, death, by his blood.

Jesus announced, '...the prince of this world now stands condemned' (Jn 16:11). Jesus has defeated the powers of darkness.

During World War II, the Allies landed on the beaches of Normandy on D-day. Both the Allies and the Nazis knew that the next twenty-four hours would settle the outcome of the conflict. The Allies won. D-day settled the war effort. Yet much bloodshed, battles and many months lay ahead before the war stopped on VE-day: Victory in Europe day. We live between two ages. God's D-day took place on the cross of Jesus. God's final V-day will happen when Jesus returns in power. Victory has been secured, but we've still got battles to fight. We move forward in the prayer war effort, not to victory but *from* victory. We advance on the basis of what Jesus has accomplished. J. O. Fraser was a missionary in China whose ministry was revolutionised when he realised this. He said, 'Deliverance from the power of the evil one comes through definite resistance on the ground of the cross.'

How can we be overcomers in the prayer war effort?

BILL HOGG'S...GUIDE TO PRAYING

'They overcame him (ie, the Enemy) *by the blood of the Lamb* and by the word of their testimony; they did not love their lives so much as to shrink from death' (Rev 12:11, italics mine).

The blood of Jesus silences the accuser. The blood of Jesus guarantees our forgiveness and acceptance. We can live in the good of that old song: 'I'm forgiven! Now I've got a reason for living. Jesus keeps giving and giving, Giving 'till my heart overflows.'

Wesley wrote this tremendous truth: 'His blood can make the foulest clean. His blood avails (ie, works) for me!'

We can make Wesley's verse our own testimony and declaration.

No condemnation now I dread.
Jesus and all in Him is mine.
Alive in Him, my living Head,
And clothed in righteousness divine.
Bold I approach the eternal throne
And claim the crown through Christ my own.

Good news! Because Jesus shed his blood we can enjoy forgiveness and acceptance. We have right of access to the Father every time we pray! We can be overcomers who enjoy protection and victory.

Revelation 12:11 contains two other key prayer ingredients: the word of your testimony, declaring the truth as you pray; and being expendable. Expendable? Yes! Someone who does not cling to his own life, but who lives as a living sacrifice!

You will experience tremendous struggles and resistance as you pray. But you don't have to settle for being a loser. Christian rock duo DeGarmo and Key remind us in their song that: 'We're destined to win. Surrounded by his love and guarded by his power, we are destined to win!'

Shadow prayer

On my knees in the night
Behind the enemy line.
On the horizon a distant fight
Defying protocol and time.

Demon hordes in the shadow
Retract from the approaching dawn,
Before warriors of light
Steadfastly marching on.

Guided by mortal men
In a midnight fire-fight,
Whose prayers ignite the path
For these warriors of light.

And from the shadow, solar flares
Are shooting through the sky
Like blazing meteorites, the prayers
Of people, like you and I.

Caving in the grip of fear,
The enemy's darkest ploy.
He knows the dawn is near
Through prayer fear is destroyed.

Alas, the ranks of uncountable legions
Are pushing back the night.
There will be no survivors
As bowstrings are drawn tight.

The battle line is that time
Where the shadow meets the new day.
Darkness slowly dissipates
As warriors of light march my way.

There is only one shadow
Providing refuge for the lost.
It's the shadow of my commander
Hanging bloodied on a cross.

He was tortured beyond reason
His face beaten, a ghastly sight.

His scars mark my salvation
From the shadow of my night.

I can see Him riding high
on the horizon, unafraid,
Fighting through to the cries
of those in the shadow, who have stayed,

On their knees fervently calling
behind the enemy's line,
unwavering, unfalling,
growing stronger all the time.

Now like a waterfall, a wave,
the new day has arrived
like arms reaching for a hug
waiting to be satisfied.

I reach out to embrace
this new day and my Saviour.
I can tell by His eyes,
in His sight, I've found favour.

Light floods my soul now
Like a thousand arching rainbows.
Life in the shadow,
    Death in the shadow...
Power in the shadow,
    Light in the shadow...

...the *shadow prayer!* (copyright March '88, Brent J. D.
Sheppard)

Notes

1. Winkie Pratney, *Doorways to Discipleship* (Bethany Fellowship: Minneapolis, USA, 1975), p 227.

2. Dick Eastman, *No Easy Road* (Bridge Publishing: Chepstow, 1984), pp 122–123.

3. E. W. Kenyon, *In His Presence* (Kenyon's Gospel Publishing Society: Washington, USA, 1969), pp 135, 136.

4. This illustration was related by David Pawson at a Spring Harvest celebration.

5. Nick Cuthbert in *A Guide to Evangelism*, edited by Calver, Copley, Moffett and Smith (Marshalls: Basingstoke, 1984), p 33.

6. From a Charles Wesley hymn.

7. Allan Boesak, SACC National Conference, June 1984, quoted from Garth Hewitt and Martin Wroe, *Nero's Watching Video* (Hodder: London, 1987), p 64.

8. H. B. Black, *Reflections on the Gifts of the Spirit* (New Dawn Books: Greenock, 1988), p 54.

9. Quoted from Paris Reidhead, *Getting Evangelicals Saved* (Bethany: USA, 1989), p 119.

10. *ibid*, p 114.

11. Gerard Kelly, *Rebel Without Applause* (Minstrel: Eastbourne, 1991), p 50.

12. The Warrior tape is available from BYFC, Cleobury Place, Cleobury Mortimer, Kidderminster, Worcs DY14 8JG. Trevor Gregory can also be contacted c/o

that address, or at the Evangelical Alliance London Office: Whitefield House, 186 Kennington Park Road SE11 4BT.

13. Quoted in Richard Foster, *A Celebration of Discipline* (Hodder: London, 1981), p 13.

14. John Allan, *Tell God* booklet (BYFC Publications), p 8.

15. David Bryant, *With Concerts of Prayer* (Regal Books: California, USA, 1985), Chapter 11.

16. Reinhard Bonnke, *Evangelism by Fire* (Kingsway: Eastbourne, 1989).

17. Story recounted by Clifford H. Richmond in 'Your Prayer Can Shake the World' from *Prayer: Its Deeper Dimensions* (Marshall, Morgan & Scott: 1963).

18. Arthur Wallis, *In the Day of Thy Power* (CLC: 1956), p 45.

19. The video segments referred to are part of a video produced for the *Mission Scotland* Youth Committee by Andy Thornton. It can be obtained from Frontier Youth Trust, 11 Queens Crescent, Glasgow G4 9AS, telephone 041–332 7208

20. Arthur Wallis, *op cit*.

21. John Dawson, *Taking Our Cities For God* (Creation House: Florida, USA, 1989), pp 18ff.

22. See Luther's hymn: 'A safe stronghold our God is still.' He tells us:

But for us fights the Proper Man,
Whom God Himself hath bidden.
Ask ye: Who is this same? Christ Jesus is his name,
The Lord Sabaoth's Son; He and no other one,
Shall conquer in the battle.

If British Youth For Christ can be of service to you, please contact:

British Youth For Christ
Cleobury Place
Cleobury Mortimer
Kidderminster
Worcs DY14 8JG
(0299) 270260

BYFC Scotland
PO Box 5
Greenock
PA16 9AS

Aids And You

by Dr Patrick Dixon

With each year that passes more and more people know someone with AIDS. People with AIDS are often young, and illness is not their only problem.... Prospects of housing, employment, insurance and even friendship can change rapidly.

—If you're still unsure about what AIDS can do
—If you've lost a friend, or fear that you may do soon

then this book will speak to you in a direct and no-nonsense way.

PATRICK DIXON is a doctor and church leader with many years' experience of caring for the dying. He is the Director of ACET—AIDS Care Education and Training—and author of the highly acclaimed book *The Truth About AIDS*.

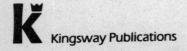

Kingsway Publications

The Occult And You

by Roger Ellis

Witches, horoscopes, ouija boards, reincarnation...

Day by day our senses are bombarded by occult propaganda; books on spiritism, newspaper reports on the paranormal, horoscopes on the radio, while New Age is all the rage.

This book warns of the dangers of dabbling with forces beyond our control. It also shows a way out for those who have been spiritually and emotionally wounded by demonic powers.

Roger Ellis lays the groundwork for a biblical understanding of the occult and the supernatural, as well as showing us how to take a positive Christian stand in spiritual warfare.

Roger Ellis is based at the Revelation Christian Fellowship in Sussex. He is a member of the Pioneer Team, and has been a regular speaker at Spring Harvest.

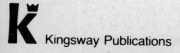

Kingsway Publications

Sex And You

by Lance Pierson

How do I keep physical love special in a world that downgrades and cheapens sex?

What has the Bible got to do with sex in the twentieth century?

How can I resist the pressure to conform when 'everybody's doing it'?

This book answers these questions—and many others—in a plain-speaking, straightforward way. It looks at the myths that the world is out to sell—and the truth of God's word which puts things in perspective.

LANCE PIERSON has been a teacher and Scripture Union worker. Thousands of young people have appreciated his honest, sympathetic approach to sexual problems and questions. He is married with two children.

'Easy to read, honest, humorous in an appropriate way, explicit but without stepping across the line into being pornographic...an excellent springboard from which parents can enter into discussion about relationships with their children.'   —*Christian Arena*

'Readable, informative...never boring or prudish'.
                                        —*Church of England Newspaper*

'I would certainly recommend young people to read this book; it might not be a bad idea for parents also!'
                                        —*Solid Rock*

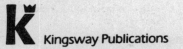

Kingsway Publications